The Koreas

GLOBALIZING REGIONS

Globalizing Regions offers concise accounts of how the nations and regions of the world are experiencing the effects of globalization. Richly descriptive yet theoretically informed, each volume shows how individual places are navigating the tension between age-old traditions and the new forces generated by globalization.

The Koreas

CHARLES K. ARMSTRONG

Routledge
Taylor & Francis Group
New York   London

Routledge is an imprint of the
Taylor & Francis Group, an informa business

Routledge
Taylor & Francis Group
270 Madison Avenue
New York, NY 10016

Routledge
Taylor & Francis Group
2 Park Square
Milton Park, Abingdon
Oxon OX14 4RN

© 2007 by Charles K. Armstrong
Routledge is an imprint of Taylor & Francis Group, an Informa business

Printed in the United States of America on acid-free paper
10 9 8 7 6 5 4 3 2 1

International Standard Book Number-10: 0-415-94853-3 (Softcover) 0-415-94852-5 (Hardcover)
International Standard Book Number-13: 978-0-415-94853-1 (Softcover) 978-0-415-94852-4 (Hardcover)

**Visit the Taylor & Francis Web site at
http://www.taylorandfrancis.com**

**and the Routledge Web site at
http://www.routledge-ny.com**

For Mira and Sara

Contents

Acknowledgments

David McBride has been as helpful, critical, and patient an editor as one could hope for.

Bruce Cumings, mentor and friend, encouraged me to pursue this project from the beginning, and his own work on contemporary Korea has been a source of inspiration throughout. My students in Korean history have long served as a sounding board and, often without realizing it, as guinea pigs for the ideas and approaches that went into this book. At Columbia, I have been fortunate to work with some of the best graduate students in Korean studies in North America. I would especially like to express my appreciation to Joy Kim, George Kallander, Bonnie Kim, Charles Kim, Alyssa Park, Cheehyung Kim, Jimin Kim, Sun-Chul Kim, Se-Mi Oh, and Hwisang Cho for all I have learned from them.

The book was completed while I was on sabbatical leave in Paris, and I am grateful to Alan Brinkley, Provost of Columbia, and Danielle Haase-Dubosc, Executive Director of Columbia's Reid Hall in Paris, for giving me the opportunity to be a scholar-in-residence there. While in Paris I also gave a series of lectures on the Koreas at the Ecole des hautes études en sciences sociales (EHESS), which helped to refine many of my ideas as I finalized the manuscript. I believe it is a better book as a result of the feedback and criticism I received at EHESS, and for that I would like to thank my hosts at the Centre de recherches sur la Corée of EHESS, Profs. Alexandre Guillemoz and Alain Delissen.

My family, as always, showed great patience and humor as I pursued a project that—again, as always—took more time and energy than I had expected. Although trained as a historian, I have written a book that is largely about the present, and points toward the future. Therefore I dedicate this book to my two daughters, who will see much more of the future than I will.

Preface

When Routledge approached me with the suggestion that I write a short book on Korea and globalization, I was intrigued, and also under the mistaken impression that "shorter" meant "easier." This turned out to be far from the case, and as I progressed in the project, I realized how difficult it was to compress a rich and complex modern history into a brief, accessible form. Korea in modern times has been at the center of global transformations like no other place on earth. From colonialism to the Cold War, capitalist industrialization to totalitarian involution, "Third Wave" democratization to the Internet revolution, the Korean peninsula has experienced world-altering events with unique intensity and in an extraordinarily compressed space and time frame. To understand how the world has changed Korea, and vice versa, and to express this with concision and clarity while still conveying the richness and complexity of Korea's interaction with the modern world, was the challenge I faced in writing this book. Whether or not I have succeeded in meeting that challenge is up to the reader to judge. But as events in and around the Korean peninsula continue to prove, the world still needs to understand Korea, and the "Korea problem" needs to be resolved once and for all. I hope to have made a small contribution to that understanding.

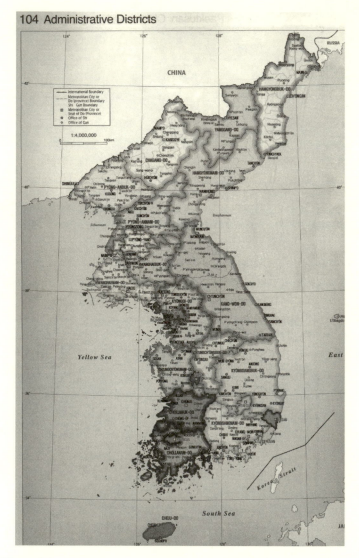

Figure 1.1
Modern-day Korea.

One

Korea in the World

England knows nothing of Korea. Yet Korea is worth knowing. It focuses so many problems, focuses them so clearly.

H.B. Drake, *Korea of the Japanese* **(1930)**[1]

Korea today exemplifies the possibilities and contradictions of globalization to a degree matched by few other places in the world. Two separate states, both products of the Cold War, confront each other on the Korean peninsula with the threat of mutual destruction long after the Cold War's end. One is an isolated, impoverished, heavily armed, and highly nationalistic Marxist-Leninist regime; the other is a burgeoning liberal democracy and emerging advanced economy deeply embedded in global networks of political, economic, and cultural interaction and integration. Coming out of a common history, culture, and ethnic identity, the two Koreas have responded to the challenge of globalization in radically different ways: North Korea appears to have resisted the global capitalist economy almost to the point of self-destruction, while South Korea is often seen as the twentieth century's most successful example of a third-world country benefiting from globalization to achieve advanced industrial status. Yet, contrary to conventional wisdom at the end of the Cold War, the successful economic and political development of South Korea, in stark contrast to the dismal economic performance and political atavism of North Korea, has not led to the absorption of the latter into the former, along the lines of German unification. North Korea, despite the enormous suffering of its people in recent decades, has proved remarkably resilient, and by the turn of the millennium had begun tentatively opening up its economy to the outside world. South Korea, especially after the financial crisis of 1997 poured cold water on its economic "miracle," has rejected the German model of unification by absorption as far too expensive and disruptive for its own interests. The two Koreas may be with us for some time to come.

As any cursory glance at the map will reveal, Korea is situated at the nexus of strategic interest among the world's most militarily powerful states (the United States, China, and Russia) and between the world's second-largest and fastest-growing national economies (Japan and China). South Korea itself is the world's tenth-largest economy, and North Korea, despite its poverty, has one of the world's largest armies and a nascent nuclear weapons program. Potential site of international war or national unification, victim of famine and major exporter of advanced technology, the Koreas are an ideal vantage point from which to observe and understand contemporary global trends and processes. In analyzing the world's impact on Korea and Korea's impact on the world, this book will consider the shifting and multiple meanings of "Korea" in contemporary history: a geographical entity, an ethnic nation, two states since 1948, and an ethno-cultural identity extending beyond the Korean peninsula to include substantial minority communities in China, the United States, Japan, and the former Soviet Union. We will seek to understand Korea's place in the world through a rigorous and historically grounded analysis of the meaning of globalization in this specific locale. While various forms of global integration have existed for millennia, the speed, scale, and depth of contemporary (post-1945, and especially post-1973) economic, political, and cultural transformations do indeed represent a new form of worldwide interconnectedness.[2] In many ways, Korea is an exemplary site for examining these transformations. For example, the migration of Koreans abroad—equivalent to 10 percent of the population of the peninsula—and the emergence of two Korean states are both products of Korea's sometimes difficult encounter with modern globalization. Divided and diasporic Korea thus forms a useful lens through which to view the modern transformation of our increasingly globalized world.

Globalization and Korea

By the beginning of the twenty-first century, "globalization" had become a nearly ubiquitous term in scholarly and popular discourses, in fields ranging from economics to international relations to cultural studies. South Korea (the Republic of Korea, ROK) in the early 1990s even established an official "globalization policy" for the country under the slogan *segyehwa* (literally "world-ization," something like the French *mondialisation*), promulgated by then-President Kim Young Sam.[3] Inevitably, such widespread usage has led to numerous and diverse definitions for this term. One of the most useful and concise definitions of globalization may be found in David Held et al., *Global Transformation*:

> Globalization can be taken to refer to those spatio-temporal processes of change which underpin a transformation in the organization of human affairs by linking together and expanding human activity across regions and continents.[4]

By this definition, globalization is nothing new; such processes have existed since the beginning of human civilization. What is new is the rapid acceleration and intensification of these processes in the last one hundred years, and especially the last fifty.

Placing Korea in world-historical time, we can see that Korea has fared differently according to different periods of globalization. If we follow Held et al. in historicizing globalization into pre-modern (to 1500), early modern (1500–1800), modern (1850–1945), and contemporary (since 1945) periods, it is evident that Korea did rather well in the first two periods. Early modern Korea, that is, the Chosŏn dynasty (1392–1910), was for much of its history a stable, peaceful, and relatively prosperous state by world standards. But Korea clashed disastrously with forces of modern globalization from the mid-nineteenth century onward. In the last half of the nineteenth century and the beginning of the twentieth, Korea lost its traditional security and trade relationship with China, declined economically and disintegrated politically, and was colonized by Japan in 1910. Liberation from Japanese colonial rule in 1945 resulted in joint Soviet-American occupation of the peninsula, leading to the creation of two separate states in 1948; this was followed in short order by a brutal civil war (1950–1953), which, because of Korea's position in the newly emerging Cold War, drew in the United States, China, and (indirectly) the Soviet Union. The war concluded with an armistice that left Korea divided, a situation that persists to this day.

Over more than half a century of separation, the two Koreas have developed into radically different political, economic, social, and cultural systems, locked in fierce competition with one another. During that time, however, their relative positions in the world system have shifted dramatically. If we divide the period of post-World War II contemporary globalization at about the mid-1970s, a key point of rupture and transformation in the global economy—the end of the gold standard, the OPEC oil shocks, the beginning of the high-tech revolution—it becomes clear that until that point, North Korea was well ahead of the South economically, as well as much more stable politically. From the mid-1970s onward, however, the South developed rapidly and soon overtook the North. By the mid-1990s the gap had grown overwhelmingly in the South's favor, and the ROK had entered the ranks of advanced industrial economies while North Korea faced a crisis of famine and de-industrialization.[5] South Korea, deeply integrated into the world system, flourished despite the setbacks of the late 1990s. North Korea, claiming stubborn adherence to a policy of *juche*, or self-reliance, staved off catastrophe largely through foreign assistance.

Thus, while Korea as a whole was undeniably a victim of modern globalization, the two Koreas since 1945 have had quite different experiences with new forms of global change: North Korea did relatively well in the first phase, South Korea did much better in the second, post-1973, phase of contemporary globalization. It is important, however, to place the more recent experience of the two Koreas in the history of Korea's overall experience of modernity since the mid-nineteenth century encounter with Europe, America, and a rising Japan, in order to understand why the two Koreas dealt so differently with the modern world. While the forces the two Korean states have had to deal with are universal, the means of dealing with them are in some ways distinct to Korea, and come out of Korea's very specific history. By the same token, the endgame of divided Korea may be quite unexpected to those who assume Korea will follow a straightforward Western path. Along the way, it is important to discard, or at least examine very critically, the widely held perception (held not least by Koreans themselves) that Korea has always been the helpless victim of foreign powers and interests.

Korea's Collision with Modernity, 1850–1953

Korea is often understood to be the natural and perennial victim of its location, a small nation caught between the rivalries of larger neighbors, a "shrimp crushed between whales," as the Korean proverb puts it. One popular study of contemporary Korean history recounts that "Korea has suffered nine hundred invasions ... in its two thousand years of recorded history."[6] This is a dubious reading of Korean history, for several reasons. First, not every attack on the Korean peninsula in recorded history can be considered an "invasion" of "Korea."

The establishment of Chinese-controlled garrisons in the northwest of the peninsula around the time of Christ cannot be seen as offenses against Korean sovereignty, as there was no such unified political or cultural unit as Korea until long afterward. In later centuries, pirate raids originating from the Japanese islands (not necessarily conducted by natives of those islands) were disruptive to life on the peninsula, but were hardly wars of conquest.

Second, compared to many other areas of the world, including much of Europe as well as other parts of East Asia, what is remarkable about Korea's history is not the number of foreign invasions, but Korea's ability to maintain internal stability and political independence over such long periods of time. If the number of attacks by foreign entities determines the degree of a state's "victimization," then China, which was conquered more often and attacked far more frequently than Korea before the twentieth century, would be the greater victim. Indeed, in the thousand years from the beginning of the Koryŏ dynasty in the tenth century to Japanese colonization in the twentieth, there were only three full-scale attempts by outside powers to conquer Korea: by the Mongols in the thirteenth century, the Japanese in the late sixteenth century, and the Japanese again the early twentieth. Only the final attack succeeded in eliminating Korean sovereignty. The Mongols made Korea a tributary of the Yuan dynasty but did not absorb Korea into their empire. The Japanese invaders of 1592–1597, led by the warlord Toyotomi Hideyoshi, were defeated by a combined force of Korean defenders and their Ming Chinese allies, although not until after the Japanese had laid waste to much of the peninsula. The Manchus of the Northeast Asian mainland also attacked Korea in the early seventeenth century, but in order to force the Korean king's shift of allegiance from the Ming to the Manchu (Qing) dynasty as the legitimate rulers of China, not to conquer Korea. It took Japanese colonization in 1910 to erase Korea's independent existence, for the first time since the peninsula had been unified in the seventh century. Few states in Asia, to say nothing of medieval and modern Europe, can claim such a record of continuous integrity and independence.

The third and most important reason that it is misleading to read Korea's history as a history of victimization due to the peninsula's unfortunate location, is that such a view ignores the historically contingent nature of geographical significance. Geography is never a "given," as spatial conceptions change with time.[7] Locations only become "strategic" at certain conjunctures of power, knowledge, and technology. For most of their history, Koreans did not at all see themselves as inhabiting a small peninsula strategically situated between rival Great Powers. A Korean map of the world in 1402 AD, for example, shows a large and centrally located China, flanked by a Korean peninsula only slightly smaller, and a tiny Japanese archipelago almost off the edge of the map (see Figure 1.2). This exemplifies the "classical" Korean view of Korea's place in the world for over a millennium: China as the central civilization, Korea nearly co-equal with China, and Japan small and insignificant.

What changed at the end of nineteenth century was the emergence of a new nexus of power, knowledge, and technology that gave rise to a stronger and more assertive Japan, and ultimately reduced Korea and China to colonial or semi-colonial status. This was a new way of envisioning and controlling the

Figure 1.2
Korean map of the world, 1402 AD

world's spaces, first articulated in Europe (especially England and Germany) and later adopted enthusiastically by the Japanese. It was a military advisor from Germany, Major Jacob Meckel, who originally suggested to the Japanese government in the 1880s that Korea was "a dagger pointed at the heart of Japan."[8] For Japanese leaders of the Meiji era (1868–1912), the Korean peninsula was of new and vital strategic importance, and had to be kept out of the hands of geopolitical rivals—first China, then Russia. This sense of geopolitical rivalry on the part of the Japanese, the desire to control spaces that might otherwise come under the domination of competitors, is quite different from the desire to drive through Korea to become emperor of China, which had motivated Hideyoshi in the 1590s. Korea, in short, fell victim to the rise of geopolitics in the final quarter of the nineteenth century.[9] It was at this point that Korea became a "shrimp among whales," a vortex of Great Power conflict. Korea was the central focus of two wars in the decade surrounding the turn of the twentieth century: the Sino-Japanese War of 1894–1895, and the Russo-Japanese War of 1904–1905. Japan won both wars, and annexed Korea in 1910.

If peace, stability, and political integrity are considered positive attributes, then Chosŏn dynasty Korea was a remarkably successful polity. The dynasty itself lasted for more than five hundred years, from 1392 to 1910. Although there have been symbolic monarchies that have lasted longer—the Japanese imperial family, for example, claims a rulership of two thousand years, but for much of that time the emperor was a powerless figurehead in Kyoto—no other actively ruling monarchy since, perhaps, ancient Egypt, has remained in power as long. But the longevity of Korean kingship is more impressive than the Chosŏn dynasty alone: the transition from the previous Koryŏ dynasty (918–1392) to Chosŏn was not a radical break, but a relatively smooth transfer of power that retained most of the institutional structure and a large part of the elite personnel from one dynasty into the next.[10] No significant interregnum or civil war separated the two. In short, the traditional Korean "political system" existed almost unchanged, with only minor adjustments, for almost exactly one thousand years.

What explains this remarkable stability and longevity? Stability does not equal stagnation. Korea did change over time, and in the seventeenth century underwent a significant rise in commercial activity, centered around the ginseng and rice merchants of the former Koryŏ capital of Kaesŏng. But social and economic change did not lead to drastic changes in the political system, or in Korea's relations with its neighbors, through much of the second millennium CE. Internally, the

Korean monarchy and bureaucracy were able to adjust them-selves to each other in a rough balance of power, and to keep under control an occasionally restive, predominantly peasant population.[11] The Korean social structure, highly stratified and unequal like most agrarian societies in history, managed to function fairly well and with few internal threats; until the nineteenth century, violent, large-scale peasant rebellions were much rarer in Korea than in China or Japan. As for Korea's external relations, after the disaster of the Japanese invasions, Chosŏn kept foreign interaction to a minimum. But even before that, Korea's interactions with its neighbors were less than vig-orous by Western standards. Korea's relations with the outside world, which meant primarily China but included Japan and "barbarian" groups in Manchuria, drew maximum advantage at minimum cost. Japan was kept at arm's length, primarily for trade relations, with a small outpost of Japanese merchants residing in the area of Pusan and occasional diplomatic mis-sions via the island of Tsushima. Chosŏn exchanged envoys three or four times a year with China and gave lip service to Chinese suzerainty, but for the most part acted independently. Barbarians to the North were generally kept in check, with Chinese assistance, or absorbed into the Korean population. As for the rest of the world, Koreans had no use whatsoever. Those few Westerners who happened to land on Korean shores, such as Dutch sailors shipwrecked on Cheju Island in the seventeenth century, were treated with respect and curios-ity but were not seen as sources of any important knowledge (unlike the Dutch colony in Japan, which was a vital source of Western or "Dutch" learning during Japan's long isolation).[12] The Korean ideal was a self-contained, self-sufficient agrarian society led by enlightened Confucian scholar-bureaucrats.[13] While Korea never entirely attained this ideal, there were few if any prominent thinkers before the late nineteenth century who disagreed with it.

The problem with such an approach to the world, is that it works relatively well so long as the world is willing to remain at arm's length. It becomes much more difficult to sustain when the world is banging on Korea's door, as the Western imperial powers were in the mid-nineteenth century. Euro-American military expansionism, missionary zeal, and commercial enterprise were impossible for Koreans to resist with traditional methods, although they certainly made an attempt. American and French incursions into Korean territorial waters in the 1860s and 1870s were successfully fought off, despite the overwhelming military might of the Western countries—Korea was simply not a prize worthy of much sacrifice, as far as most Europeans and Americans were concerned. Other parts of Asia—India, Indochina, the Philippines, not to mention the vast markets and resources of China itself—preoccupied Western interests in the latter nineteenth century. Korean recalcitrance earned it the nickname "Hermit Kingdom"; Westerners, for the most part, shrugged their shoulders at these peculiarly isolated and stubborn people and moved on. However, this apparent success at resisting Western aggression lulled Korean elites into a false sense of security. When a foreign power came along that was truly determined to open up Korea to Western-style diplomacy and commerce—in this case, a rapidly westernizing Japan in 1875—Korean isolation could not be maintained. Japan signed the first modern diplomatic treaty with Korea in 1876, and other countries soon followed. The Hermit Kingdom was isolated no more, and the Chosŏn dynasty itself would collapse after a few short decades.

In many ways, the Japanese were typical colonial rulers in the European model of the late nineteenth and early twentieth centuries. Japanese citizens—businessmen, bureaucrats, teachers, farmers, soldiers—lived privileged lives in occupied Korea, mostly in Japanese communities and neighborhoods in large cities such as Seoul, Pyongyang, Pusan, and Taegu. Like other colonial subjects, Koreans became second-class citizens in their own country. At the apex of the colonial governing system was the Governor-General, who ruled as a virtual dictator, largely independent of control from Tokyo. Whatever benefits Koreans derived from Japanese colonial rule, a subject of considerable and heated debate between the countries even today, came about as side effects of policies intending to help Japan.[14]

Some aspects of the Korean colonial experience, however, were atypical. The proximity of Korea to Japan gave the colony a direct strategic significance much greater than that of India to Britain, say, or the East Indies to the Netherlands. Regarding their Korean colonial subjects, the Japanese spoke a rhetoric of cultural similarity and (at times) assimilation, at least in contrast to the West, even though the long history of cultural difference and distinction between Japan and Korea was obvious for all to see. The Japanese colonial bureaucracy was unusually large, very much biased toward Japanese at the upper levels, and pervaded Korean society to a degree few if any other colonial powers matched. Perhaps most unusually of all, from the late 1920s onward Japanese authorities put a concerted effort into industrializing Korea. In the 1930s and early 1940s, Korea became a key part of a regional imperial economy centered on Japan, and extending into Manchuria, China proper, and, with the onset of the Pacific War, into Southeast Asia. The results for Koreans were mixed. On the one hand, parts of the Korean peninsula became relatively industrialized, particularly in the North, with its abundant mineral resources and hydroelectric power potential. On the other hand, most Koreans experienced the industrialization process in the context of a highly oppressive war mobilization, which pressed Koreans into labor in new factories in Korea as well as in Japan, not to mention drafting Korean men into military service and tens of thousands of Korean women and girls into sexual slavery for the Japanese army. At the end of World War II, Korea could be considered the most industrialized country in Asia after Japan itself, but the Korean people had paid a heavy price, and not through any choice of their own, to attain that status.

Korea's liberation by the two leading World War II allies, the Soviet Union and the United States, was greeted with euphoria by the Koreans, but soon created new problems. The peninsula was arbitrarily divided at the thirty-eighth parallel, an American proposal intended to expedite the surrender of Japanese forces on the peninsula (and to ensure an American role in Korea before the Soviets could occupy the entire country unilaterally). Soviet leader Joseph Stalin agreed with the American proposal. Koreans were not consulted in this joint occupation policy, but no one—Americans, Soviets, or Koreans—expected the division to last very long. Unfortunately, Korea was almost immediately caught up in a new geopolitical struggle, this time between the two occupation powers over spheres of interest and conflict in Europe, the Middle East, and Asia. The Cold War combined geopolitical competition with ideological rivalry; the left-right split within Korean domestic politics, rooted in the colonial period, inexorably fused with the policies of the two rival occupation powers.[15] Three meetings between Soviet and American officials to establish a framework for a unified Korean government ended in failure. By early 1946, there were already two de facto governments on the peninsula: one in the south, headed by the American-educated independence leader Syngman Rhee and backed by the United States; and the other in the north, dominated by communists, supported by Moscow, and led by Kim Il Sung, a young veteran of the guerilla struggle against the Japanese in Manchuria who had joined the Soviet Far Eastern Army in the final years of World War II. In August 1948, after a UN-backed election boycotted by the North and the Soviets, the Republic of Korea (ROK) was established in Seoul. Three weeks later, on September 9th, the Democratic People's Republic of Korea (DPRK) was declared in Pyongyang. Both regimes claimed sovereignty over the entire peninsula. Given such mutually exclusive claims, war was virtually inevitable; the only question was which side, South or North, would start it.

The answer came on June 25, 1950, when the Korean People's Army attacked the South to reunify the peninsula by force. The attack had been considered for well over a year, since Kim Il Sung had first proposed to Stalin that, given the current balance of forces in the North's favor, military conquest of the South would be relatively swift and cost-effective, forcing the Americans to accept a Communist fait accompli.[16] Circumstances, however, did not evolve quite as Kim had predicted. The Americans did intervene, pushing the North Korean forces back well above the thirty-eighth parallel, and provoking a Chinese counter-intervention. The result, after the Chinese entered the war in late October 1950, and had pushed the Americans in turn south of the thirty-eighth parallel by

January 1951, was two-and-a-half years of brutal stalemate. Finally, in July 1953, the People's Republic of China, North Korea, and the United Nations Command signed an armistice to end the fighting. A De-Militarized Zone (DMZ) was established, running close to the initial thirty-eighth parallel line, to separate North and South. After three years of fighting, millions of casualties, and untold physical destruction, the Korean War ended approximately where it had begun, and Korea remained more bitterly divided than ever.

In point of technical fact, the Korean War did not end in July 1953. The belligerent parties signed a truce, a temporary secession of hostilities, and hopes for a more permanent solution to the end the Korean conflict never materialized. Instead, two mutually hostile Korean regimes armed themselves to the teeth in case of renewed hostilities on the peninsula, and competed fiercely for the loyalty of Koreans on the other side of the DMZ, as well as for recognition in the international community.[17] By the early 1960s, both Korean regimes were supported by mutual defense treaties with their respective Great Power patrons—the United States for South Korea, the Soviet Union and China for the North. If open hostilities between the two Koreas had broken out again, this may very well have led to a nuclear war between two of the major Cold War antagonists. For decades, the near-symmetrical conflict on the Korean peninsula neatly reflected the duality of the Cold War: a zero-sum political and strategic antagonism buttressed by ideological opposition. Korea, like Germany and Vietnam, was a "divided nation in a divided world," in the memorable phrase of a noted Korea expert.[18]

But the division of Korea long outlasted the end of the Cold War in 1989–1991, when the example of German unification seemed to presage Korea's near future. As I will argue, Korea's continued division is not merely an epiphenomenon of the Cold War, even though the Cold War created the circumstances that made this division possible. Rather, the two Koreas represent a much deeper divide in modern world history: opposed approaches to fundamental questions of political independence, economic development, and governance that all societies have had to face in adjusting to the disruptive changes of modernity. The Koreas, in other words, reflect two possible and legitimate outcomes of Korea's collision with the modern world, and more generally the pressing issues of developing nations throughout the long twentieth century, one whose solution—despite the seemingly unstoppable march of market capitalism and liberal democracy at the turn of the millennium—remains in question.

Common history and hopes for unification notwithstanding, it is obvious that North and South Korea are in fact two different states and societies. Thus, although it is important to appreciate the proximity of the two Koreas to each other and the antagonistic interdependence in which they have developed since 1948, the radically different ways they have dealt with the world and with their own domestic development are worth examining separately. Chapter 2 looks at South Korea, and traces its emergence from an unstable and deeply corrupt dependency of the United States to a regional and global economic force in its own right, successfully exporting advanced technology and its own popular culture, while simultaneously transforming itself from a highly authoritarian, military-dominated regime to a civilian democracy. Chapter 3 examines North Korea, which has taken a very different approach to the same questions of development and global interaction, and has consequently followed a very different trajectory: from socialist economic showcase in the 1950s to economic catastrophe in the 1990s, insisting on charting its own idiosyncratic course in the world, while maintaining a political regime that has been deeply undemocratic at best, and whose human rights record is among the worst in the world.

Another product of Korea's collision with modernity is the migration of Koreans beyond the peninsula, which was almost nonexistent before the second half of the nineteenth century. Emigration was accelerated by Japanese colonial rule, war mobilization, and industrialization, and by the end of World War II millions of Koreans lived abroad, mostly in China, Japan, and the Soviet Union. More recently, large numbers of Koreans have migrated from South Korea to the United States, making the Korean American community the largest in the Korean diaspora. Chapter 4 discusses the history of these overseas Korean communities, and their varied connections to and identifications with the peninsular "homeland."

With Chapter 5, we return to the seemingly intractable Korean conflict to try to explain its longevity and speculate on its potential outcome. On the one hand, the two Koreas remain locked in mutual antagonism and an armed truce, prepared at all times for war with each other. On the other hand, there have been periodic movements since the early 1970s toward reconciliation between the two Korean states, and since the South Korean administration of Kim Dae Jung came to power in 1998, South Korea has made engagement with the North a priority. The complexity of Korea's division stems from the fact that Koreans alone are not free to decide how to resolve it. At least four other, more powerful, nations have a direct stake in the Korean issue: China, Japan, Russia, and the United States.

The latter has focused much of its attention since the early 1990s on the North Korean "nuclear issue," the (potential or real) development of nuclear weapons by North Korea, which the United States views essentially as an enemy country. Various agreements and negotiation frameworks were attempted to resolve the nuclear issue, but for over a decade it remained the key point of conflict between the United States and the DPRK, with potentially ominous repercussions for other regional players, above all South Korea. At the beginning of the twenty-first century, Korea remains one of the few places in the world that could trigger a full-scale war among major powers. The "Korean Question," which has been a concern of the international community since the end of the nineteenth century and the focus of three wars by the mid-twentieth, is still very much with us today. Its outcome, whether peaceful or violent, will have profound and far-reaching implications for Korea, the East Asian region, and the world.

Modern Korean history has been, on the whole, a history of relative weakness, with many of the fundamental questions of Korea's future having been decided by outside powers. Indeed, the entire history of Korea from the beginning of the twentieth century to the present is one of either colonial domination or national division. But this victimization is not an eternal, natural fact of Korean history. By the beginning of the twenty-first century, (South) Korea was reemerging as an important country in East Asia and the world. A leading exporting and high-tech nation, a population of forty-six million in the South alone, and a peninsular population of nearly seventy million, not to mention some five million émigrés and their descendents, is not a force that can be easily ignored. A unified Korea could make a far greater impact on the world even than South Korea today. If the most critical issues of conflict in and around the Korean peninsula are resolved peacefully and productively, Korea's place in the world will be very different in the twenty-first century than it was in the twentieth.

Two

South Korea: The Rise to Globalism

UNDER THE AMERICAN UMBRELLA

When the fighting ended in July 1953, the De-Militarized Zone (DMZ), established to separate the two warring sides of the Korean conflict, ran like a jagged scar across the body of the peninsula. One either side of the line lay little but devastation and misery. Seoul, the capital of the Republic of Korea in the South, was in ruins, having been taken and retaken four times in the course of the war. Most cities in the North had been flattened by the American bombing. The infrastructure of industrial life—roads, train lines, bridges, dams, factories, power plants—had been largely destroyed. Millions of Koreans had been killed, maimed, or made homeless as a result of the war. Most of those who remained alive were overwhelmed by the struggle for sheer survival. A comfortable quality of life, much less world-class affluence, could hardly even be dreamt.

South Korea after the war was one of the least promising places in the world for economic development. Cut off from the rich mineral and power resources of the North, South Korea was at best an island of agricultural subsistence. Much of its population was barely literate. Its middle class, such as it was, was miniscule and compromised by collaboration with Japan, the losers of World War II. An observer of post-colonial Asia would likely have predicted that Burma, a country similar in size to Korea but with far greater natural resource endowments, ample land for rice production, and an English-educated elite, was much better positioned than South Korea to move upward in the world economy.[1]

If its economic prospects seemed dismal, South Korea showed even less promise in the area of politics. Emerging from decades of a highly militarized Japanese colonialism, preceded by centuries of Neo-Confucian monarchy, Koreans had had little if any exposure to democratic ideas and practices. Democracy was a recent imposition of the Americans, poorly attuned to Korea's traditions, and in any case had not been imposed with much care or enthusiasm. South Korea's inevitable fate appeared to be that of an impoverished dictatorship, dependent on U.S. aid for the foreseeable future. But to the astonishment of much of the world, South Korea ultimately escaped this grim fate. By the 1990s, it was Burma that had become an impoverished, militarized dictatorship and a pariah to much of the Western world. North Korea, which had showed greater promise in the economic realm than had the South in the early postwar years (as will be discussed in the following chapter), had fallen far behind South Korea economically, and was even more politically barren than Burma. Many internal and historical factors, not least the legacies of

Japanese colonial rule, shaped the postwar transformation of South Korea from a war-devastated backwater to a modern industrial democracy in the space of a single generation. But the indispensable and inescapable context of this transformation was South Korea's position in the postwar world system, which is to say, its role as a frontline state in the Cold War, beneath the umbrella of American aid and protection.

The Republic of Korea (ROK) benefited from having as its patron the richest and most militarily powerful country on earth, a country that pumped enormous economic resources into sustaining South Korea, and committed itself to the defense and political viability of the republic. Of course, American support alone would not have ensured the long-term existence, much less economic and political success, of the ROK; South Vietnam is a glaring example of American failure in the East Asian region, and the record of the Philippines, another American dependency in Asia, is decidedly mixed. But the United States established the environment within which Koreans effected first an economic "miracle," followed by a breakthrough to sustainable democracy.

As far as military security was concerned, the United States was responsible for the very survival of the ROK, which would have lost the war to the North in 1950 without American intervention. The subsequent American defense commitment helped prevent a renewed attack from North Korea, although without going so far as to support a South Korean attack against the North, as Syngman Rhee may have wanted. From 1958 to 1991, the United States backed its defense of the ROK with nuclear weapons stationed on Korean soil. Although tactical nuclear weapons were removed under President George H. W. Bush, U.S. military doctrine maintained the threat of a "credible" nuclear retaliation to deter a North Korean attack against the South. The United States retained operational control of military forces in South Korea, through the American-led Combined Forces Command (CFC), until 1994, when peacetime control was ceded to the ROK military. In the event of war, however, the United States would assume command of these "combined" forces.[2]

Economically, South Korea was overwhelmingly dependent on American aid from the beginning of the republic in 1948, well into the era of Park Chung Hee's military-led government (1961–1979). During this time, South Korea received the largest amounts of U.S. aid per capita of any country in the world save Israel and South Vietnam.[3] In the early postwar years, more than half of ROK government spending came from American assistance. The United States also absorbed the bulk of Korea's imports, at relatively low tariff rates, until the mid-1980s. America was South Korea's financial guarantor and market of last resort; without U.S. patronage, the South Korean "economic miracle" would have emerged very differently, if at all.

Socially and culturally, the American presence was also enormous. The United States Army Military Government (USAMGIK) that ruled South Korea from 1945 to 1948 oversaw a drastic overhaul in the South Korean education system, which was rebuilt largely along American lines.[4] In the area of popular culture, South Korea was permeated by American films, music, literature, and television even more than other parts of the postwar world; in Asia, possibly only the Philippines, an outright colony of the United States for nearly half a century, was influenced as deeply by American culture as was South Korea.[5] This massive American presence encountered little overt resistance by South Koreans from the Korean War to the period of democratic transition in the mid- to late-1980s. Partly because of a widespread sense of gratitude for American involvement in the war, partly because of strongly pro-American authoritarian governments and pervasive anti-communist education, and partly because the American cultural presence was seen as preferable to Japanese popular culture (which was officially forbidden for South Korean consumption until the late 1990s), South Korea remained almost bereft of open anti-American public sentiment until the 1980s.[6] From that point onward, however, criticism of the United States became part of the landscape of Korean culture and politics.[7]

In all of these ways, except perhaps militarily, South Korea was visibly asserting its independence vis à vis the United States by the 1990s. On the economic front, a series of trade disputes between the United States and the ROK in the 1980s signified the start of dramatic changes in U.S.-Korean economic relations. From the 1980s onward Korea retained a consistent trade surplus with the United States, while the U.S. share of Korea's exports steadily fell. By 2003 China had surpassed the United States as South Korea's largest trading partner, and was also the number one destination for South Korean investment. After a drop in the late 1990s due to the Asian financial crisis, South Korea's trade surplus with the United States expanded again, to well over $10 billion. South Korea's position as an aid supplicant and dependent of the United States would seem a distant memory by the start of the new millennium.

Just as South Korea's economic dependence on the United States had declined drastically by the end of the 1990s, so had its cultural dependence. Indeed, South Korea itself has become a major exporter of popular culture products, especially music, movies, and television dramas. At the turn of the millennium, Korean pop culture became overnight, it seemed, the rage all over eastern Asia, from Japan to Vietnam, and especially in "Greater China" (Taiwan, Hong Kong, and the People's Republic).[8] In the mid-1980s, the South Korean film industry was in danger of being crushed by the Hollywood juggernaut, as regulations on American film imports were liberalized. A decade and a half later, South Korea was one of the few capitalist countries in the world in which domestic films took a higher share of box office than Hollywood films. Homemade blockbusters broke one domestic box office record after another in the late 1990s and early 2000s, and for the first time Korean movies made substantial headway into the Japanese and Chinese film markets as well. While Korean films were more popular in Asia than in the West, even American and European film critics and aficionados began to dub South Korean cinema "the new Hong Kong."[9] In movies as in automobiles and electronics, South Korea had risen from utter dependence into the ranks of leadership.

South Korea's political and military relationship with the United States had been a topic virtually off-limits to public debate from the Korean War onward. While the U.S.-ROK alliance itself was not seriously questioned by South Korean governments, or for that matter the majority of the South Korean public, the nature of the alliance became the subject of criticism and growing demands for change in the post-democracy period. "Anti-Americanism," or perhaps more accurately criticism of U.S. foreign policy in general and U.S. relations with Korea in particular, migrated from the radical fringes in the 1980s to mainstream South Korean public opinion in the 2000s. Anti-U.S. protests were triggered by certain specific events, such as the accidental killing of two Korean school-girls by American soldiers in 2002 and the U.S. invasion of Iraq in 2003; in the winter of 2002–2003, tens of thousands of Koreans poured into the streets for candlelight vigils protesting American policies and action. Such responses, however, were a reflection of a deeper shift in Korean attitudes toward the United States. Younger South Koreans in particular viewed the United States more critically than did their elders.[10] These new attitudes did not prevent South Korean students from remaining the largest group of foreign students in the United States, in proportion to the homeland population (only China and India, countries with twenty times the population of South Korea, had more students in the United States in absolute numbers), although by 2003 there were even more South Koreans studying in China than in the United States. But they did suggest that South Koreans would no longer view the United States universally as a benevolent elder brother, and that the unequal nature of the U.S.-ROK alliance, as expressed in the Status of Forces Agreement (SOFA) between the two countries' military forces, would come under scrutiny and be at some point changed.[11] While no mainstream politician could advocate terminating the U.S. military presence in South Korea outright, Lee Hoi-chang lost the 2002 presidential election in part because he was portrayed by his opponent, Roh Moo-hyun, as too pro-American. Even among South Korean conservatives, the old, reflexively pro-American political establishment was on its way out by the beginning of the new millennium. Whatever the U.S.-ROK alliance would evolve into, the patron-client dependent relationship of the previous fifty years was no longer tenable.

ECONOMIC AND POLITICAL TRANSFORMATIONS
"Korea, Inc."—1961–1985

While the U.S. umbrella provided the context in which these transformations took place, indigenous factors made such transformations possible. In the economic area, a powerful centralized state set on rapid, export-oriented modernization—the "developmental state," political scientists have called it—played the leading role.[12] South Korea's rapid industrialization, the so-called "miracle on the River Han," was a collaborative effort of government and big business, with government firmly in command.[13] This collusive model was established in the early 1960s, under the military regime of Park Chung Hee, and produced spectacular returns in GNP growth until the mid-1980s. It began to falter in the late 1980s and went through a slow, difficult transition in the 1990s. The 1997 Asian financial crisis, which threatened to undermine the entire South Korean economy, seemed to be the final blow to the Korean high-growth model. But South Korea recovered more rapidly and more completely than any of the other countries affected by the regional financial crisis. While the days of double-digit GNP growth were gone forever, the domination of the chaebŏl, or large business conglomerates, a product of the rapid industrialization period, persisted into the new millennium. South Korea seemed uncertain whether its future lay in neo-liberal free market reform or some new system of formal cooperation among business, government, and perhaps other social elements such as organized labor.[14]

This strong state was not a holdover of Korea's traditional "Oriental Despotism." During the Chosŏn dynasty (1302–1910), the central government as embodied in the king had been relatively weak vis à vis competing bureaucratic interests.[15] The Japanese colonial regime in the 1930s and early 1940s, under the virtually dictatorial control of the Governor-General, established the proximate model for South Korea's state-led industrialization.[16] Not by coincidence, the rapid industrialization process of the 1960s and 1970s, under the direction of ROK president and former Japanese imperial army officer Park Chung Hee, strikingly resembled its predecessor in wartime Japan: an authoritarian state dominated by the military; large diversified business groups or conglomerates (*zaibatsu* in Japanese, *chaebŏl* in Korean—the same Chinese characters with different pronunciations); and reliance on abundant supplies of cheap labor.[17] George E. Ogle, among others, has argued that the South Korean system of labor relations derived directly from the Japanese *sampo* system that had subordinated workers to the war effort.[18]

International factors also played an important role. In addition to the general contribution of American aid and patronage, the American war in Vietnam specifically gave a tremendous boost to the South Korean economy. The contribution of more than 300,000 Korean combat soldiers to Vietnam—by far the largest non-U.S. foreign force contribution to the war—was repaid with generous U.S. civilian and military subsidies, totaling more than one billion dollars between 1965 and 1970.[19] Perhaps more importantly in the long run, South Korea's heavy industries took off substantially due to war procurements for Vietnam. Hyundai Construction, Hanjin Transportation, and other leading conglomerates were relatively small concerns until the Vietnam War windfall. While the ROK exported primarily labor-intensive light consumer goods to the United States and Japan, it exported over 90 percent of its steel and over 50 percent of its transportation equipment to Vietnam in the late 1960s.[20] Even so, South Korea's take-off might not have been sustained after the fall of Saigon and the severing of ROK-Vietnam economic ties, had the same big businesses not moved into the next lucrative foreign market: construction in the oil-producing countries of the Middle East and North Africa. Hyundai, Daewoo, Hanjin, and other Korean companies set up factories in, and shipped tens of thousands of workers to, the newly rich but underdeveloped countries of the region, especially Saudi Arabia, Iraq, and Libya. This move was both highly profitable for these businesses and also helped secure oil supplies for South Korea's own industrialization program.

Another key external factor in this period of economic take-off was Japan. In 1965 the ROK and Japan normalized relations, despite widespread protests in South Korea. One condition of normalization was that Japan give South Korea some $800 million in compensation for damages incurred by its colonial domination, an enormous sum for South Korea at the time. South Korea was opened up to Japanese business, and in the early 1970s Japan surpassed the United States as the largest foreign investor in Korea (it was to lose that position to the United States again later). Much of South Korea's foreign technical assistance came from Japan, at a time when Japanese production was the most efficient in the world.[21] Technology transfer also played a key role. Entire industries that were declining in Japan, such as steel and shipbuilding, and entire plants for these industries, were shifted to South Korea, and the Koreans became global leaders in many of these industries.[22] Japan was important in yet another, less tangible way: as Korea's model and competitor. As a Hyundai executive who had run his company's programs in the Middle East remarked to me, "We were obsessed with beating Japan. That drove us to work harder and put all our efforts into creating the most efficient, most productive industries we could. Catching up with and surpassing Japan was our goal."

The Rise, Fall, and Recovery of the Korean Economy

The economic results of this state-led industrialization process were remarkable, even if the authoritarian nature of Park's regime was widely criticized in the outside world and faced considerable discontent within South Korea. In the 1970s, for example, GNP grew at an average annual rate of 9 percent, exports by 28 percent; heavy industry rapidly expanded its share of South Korea's economic output, from 40 percent in 1971 to 56 percent in 1980.[23] A country with a per capita income of $100 per annum in 1961, at the time of Park's coup—on par with India, less than that of Sudan, and one-third that of Mexico—had by the end of 1996 a per capita annual income of over $10,000 and was a member of the Organization of Economic Cooperation and Development, the club of rich nations based in Paris.[24] But the model began to falter in the mid-1980s, during the regime of General Chun Doo Hwan, South Korea's second successive military president.

After Chun came to power in 1980, South Korea began gradually to liberalize its economy under strong outside pressure, primarily from the United States. Korean markets were opened to U.S. imports, tariffs were relaxed somewhat, and government control of big business declined (after one last spectacular example of state power over business in 1985, when Chun refused government loans to the Kukje *chaebŏl* and the company collapsed). The 1980s were also a period of unprecedented labor disputes under the authoritarian regime, and workers' wages sharply increased even if their rights remained severely restricted. In short, the "developmental state" was losing ground to both the *chaebŏl* and to organized labor. Moreover, the Chun regime's authoritarian ways were deeply unpopular, and the government faced strong pressure from below for democratization. The loss of state power relative to both big business and popular forces for democratization continued after the fall of Chun in 1987; the growing autonomy of the *chaebŏl* in the era of democratization was perhaps most dramatically expressed in the presidential election of 1992, when Hyundai founder Chung Ju Young ran for president and won 16.1 percent of the vote.[25]

The Korean "miracle" faced its greatest challenge in late 1997, when South Korea became caught up in the financial crisis that swept through eastern Asia from Thailand, Indonesia, Malaysia, Singapore, and Hong Kong. Indonesia, Thailand, and South Korea were hit the hardest. In November, the South Korean stock market plunged, as did the value of the won; Moody's Investment Services lowered Korea's credit rating from A1 to A3; foreign reserves began to flood out of the country. In 1998, South Korea's GDP fell by nearly 7 percent. The International Monetary Fund responded with an emergency rescue package amounting to some $55 billion dollars, the largest loan in the IMF's history.[26] The role of the IMF in the Asian financial crisis was and remains controversial. Some leading economists, including Nobel laureate Joseph Stiglitz, have argued that South Korea successfully recovered precisely because it *didn't* follow all of the IMF's advice, including raising exchange rates and shedding excess capacity.[27] Whatever the case, the South Korean economy recovered faster and more fully than that of other countries hit by the crisis. The economic contraction had been completely reversed within two years: according to Bank of Korea statistics, in 1999 GDP growth was 9.5 percent, in 2000 8.5 percent, and thereafter growth remained steadily positive, at around 3 percent per annum through 2005.[28] This was a far cry from the breakneck growth of the roaring 1970s, but an impressive recovery from the near-catastrophe of the late 1990s.

As South Korea entered the new millennium, the model that had guided the country from desperate poverty to first-world affluence was undergoing fundamental revamping, a process under way long before the 1997 crisis, although that crisis brought the problems of the economic miracle into sharp focus. Koreans did not drift or decline for long; soon the country's business and government leaders were embarking on new, ambitious projects to expand further the South Korean economy for a new age of globalization and regional integration. Perhaps the most ambitious project was the plan to create a high-tech "ubiquitous city" on the island of Songdo, near the country's new Inchon International Airport, a multi-billion dollar joint venture with American firms designed to take advantage of the fast-growing economy of China just across the Yellow Sea.[29] South Korea, as always, was on the move. No country in the world has industrialized as quickly and as extensively as has the Republic of Korea. It is the first country since Japan to move from the periphery of the global economy to advanced industrial status, and did so in a single generation. On the other hand, political progress did not always coincide with economic development, and was anything but smooth.

Authoritarianism and its Discontents

If South Korea's economic prospects looked bleak in 1953, its political future looked no better. When U.S. forces occupied South Korea and helped establish Korea's first Republic in the late 1940s, Korea did not appear very promising soil for cultivating democracy. The previous thirty-five years of Japanese colonial rule had been characterized by harsh, militarized exploitation of the Korean people. Before that, Korea had been ruled for centuries by a centralized Confucian monarchy and bureaucracy, modeled on those of imperial China. In short, Korean political traditions were strongly authoritarian and elitist. These traditions persisted well into the modern period. To be sure, there was a countervailing tradition of grass-roots populism, dramatically expressed in the Tonghak ("Eastern Learning") peasant uprising of 1894–1895, and its political offshoots.[30] There were attempts at political and social reform from above during the short-lived coup of 1884 and the *Kabo* (1894) reform movement of the mid-1890s, both supported by Japan and both followed by conservative reactions. The Western-educated, American-leaning leaders of the Independence Club (1896–1898) promoted a cautious democratization within a monarchical context.[31] But Korea was barely on the road to constitutional monarchy, much less popular democracy, when Japan annexed the peninsula in 1910. Western-style democracy was viewed with suspicion by the Japanese authorities, and Soviet-style socialism, which began to attract some Koreans in the 1920s as an alternative, was ruthlessly crushed. The latter in any case was not terribly democratic to begin with, and after the Korean War any organized left-wing movement was effectively eliminated in South Korea. Despite this, the tension between an authoritarian leadership and a populist opposition remained strong for the first four decades of the Republic.

These decades were characterized by long periods of authoritarian rule punctuated by brief moments of popular upheaval, in 1960–1961 and 1979–1980. But in the late 1980s, South Korea underwent a dramatic transformation from military government to civilian democracy, beginning with the demise of the Chun Doo Hwan military regime. Unlike previous democratic breakthroughs that ended the autocratic governments of Syngman Rhee and Park Chung Hee, only to be followed by new authoritarian regimes, the democratic breakthrough of the late 1980s showed signs of permanence. In 1992, long-time opposition figure Kim Young Sam was elected the first civilian president in over thirty years, as the representative of a political coalition with the previous ruling party. In 1997, pro-democracy activist Kim Dae Jung was elected president in the first peaceful transfer of power from the ruling party to the opposition South Korea had ever experienced. In 2002, Kim's protégé Roh Moo-hyun was elected in a closely fought contest with the conservative opposition leader Lee Hoi-chang. At the beginning of the twenty-first century, despite a number of outstanding problems, democracy seemed firmly consolidated in South Korea.

The First Republic of Syngman Rhee was democratic on paper but highly authoritarian in practice. Moreover, it was seen as blatantly corrupt by much of the South Korean public. In the spring of 1960, a rigged election and a harsh crackdown on antigovernment protest triggered a series of large demonstrations that led to Rhee's resignation and exile. This event came to be known as the "April 19 Student Revolution," as students and teachers took the lead in these protests. After a year of political tumult under Prime Minister Chang Myŏn, a military coup led by Major General Park Chung Hee took control of the Republic in May 1961. Park was as authoritarian as Rhee, if not more so, but unlike Rhee he was not seen as personally corrupt, and more importantly launched South Korea on a path of rapid economic development that eventually created the "miracle on the River Han."

While Rhee's ideological vision had been largely negative—anti-communist and anti-Japanese—Park was, as we have seen, committed to a more positive vision of national wealth and power through economic development. His conscious model was Japan. A graduate of the Manchurian Military Academy and a former lieutenant in the Japanese Imperial Army, Park had been deeply impressed by Japan's strength as a military force and its rapid economic growth of the late nineteenth and early twentieth centuries. Park was especially interested in the origins of that growth in the Meiji period (1868–1912). In 1972, Park revised the ROK Constitution to give himself virtually dictatorial power, and called this new constitution the "Yushin Constitution"—Yushin ("Revitalization") being the Korean pronunciation for the same characters used in the Japanese term for the Meiji Restoration (*Meiji Ishin*).

The economic fruits of Park's developmental regime were apparent by the end of the 1960s, but Park's authoritarian ways finally led to his downfall. In the early 1970s, a series of external and internal shocks—the U.S. "Nixon Doctrine," accompanying the wind-down of American forces in Vietnam, which signaled a reduction in America's defense commitments in Asia; the OPEC oil embargo and global recession, damaging the Korean economy and helping to slow exports; and the

ROK presidential election of 1971, in which opposition leader Kim Dae Jung won over 40 percent of the vote despite Park's enormous leverage over the electoral process—weakened the political and economic bases of Park's government. Park responded by declaring martial law in 1972. Finally, Park was assassinated by his own chief of intelligence in October 1979.

Park's assassination was followed by another period of political confusion, with Prime Minister Choi Kyu-hwa playing a transitional role analogous to that of Chang Myŏn after Syngman Rhee's abdication in 1960. This time, however, the window of civilian rule was even briefer than in 1960, and within two months of Park's death, on December 12, 1979, Major General Chun Doo Hwan led a mutiny against the military leadership. Assisted by his military academy classmate Roh Tae-woo, who brought in his Ninth Army Division that guarded the invasion routes from the North, Chun's loyalists occupied strategic parts of Seoul and defeated the old regime military in a matter of hours. Still, Chun had not yet declared himself leader of the country. The hopes for democracy were high during the "Seoul Spring" of 1980, and the two major opposition leaders under Park, Kim Dae Jung and Kim Young Sam, along with Park's former crony Kim Jong Pil, attempted to rally political support behind them. But in April 1980, Chun declared himself head of the Korean Central Intelligence Agency, Park's most notorious instrument of coercion and social control, and moved the country toward martial law. Protests erupted throughout the country, especially on university campuses in Seoul and other major cities. In the southwestern provincial capital of Kwangju, Kim Dae Jung's native stronghold, Chun decided to teach the protestors a violent lesson. On May 18, the protests in Kwangju were brutally put down by elite Special Forces paratroopers. The crackdown led to a popular local response that became a full-scale insurrection, and for a few days the city of Kwangju was ruled by local citizens' councils, beyond the reach of the central government. On May 27, the army moved in. The result was a massacre whose full extent may never be known, but which resulted in as many as two thousand civilian deaths.[32] The bloody suppression in Kwangju would haunt Chun for his entire presidency.

The Democratic Breakthrough

In justifying dictatorship in the name of economic development, Park Chung Hee had once said, "Food comes before politics. Only with a full stomach can one enjoy the arts and talk about social developments."[33] As a matter of fact, South Korea had a vibrant political and cultural life long before economic take-off, even—perhaps especially—in the impoverished post-Korean War years of the mid- to late-1950s. Poverty did not prevent thousands of South Koreans publicly demanding, and attaining, the resignation of Syngman Rhee in 1960. But the protestors of the 1950s and 1960s were for the most part a small, educated minority. By the 1980s, however, the democratic movement had become much more widespread. Their stomachs now full, South Koreans in ever-increasing numbers were willing to confront the political and economic injustices of their society.

The democratic movement of the 1980s, culminating in the extraordinary events of June 1987 that brought hundreds of thousands of South Koreans into the streets to protest against the Chun Doo Hwan regime, involved a broad coalition of social groups, professions, and classes. Students, intellectuals, and religious leaders played a prominent role, as they had in earlier anti-authoritarian protests. Middle-class, white-collar professionals joined as well, with their own demands for political and economic rights, particularly unionization.[34] But constituting a critical new element in the democratic movement were the blue-collar workers, a more visible, vibrant, and militant labor force than South Korea had ever seen before. This was a direct product of the country's rapid industrialization.

A strong labor movement emerged in South Korea shortly after liberation in 1945; a left-wing umbrella organization that attempted to coordinate this movement, the National Council of Korean Trade Unions (Chŏnp'yong in its Korean abbreviation), came into sharp conflict with the U.S. military government and South Korean police. The Americans and their Korean supporters created an alternative and more pliable organization, the Federation of Korean Trade Unions (Noch'ong) in 1946. Both Rhee and Park suppressed any labor organization that attempted to be independent of state control. Under Park, however, the process of industrialization inevitably created a rapidly expanding population of factory labor workers that the government could not control except with increasing force and brutality.

If there was one event that signaled the birth of a new militant labor movement, it was the self-immolation of Chŏn T'ae-il, a young garment-factory worker, in November 1970. Chŏn set himself afire to protest the abysmal working conditions that underlay the economic miracle, and his death triggered a new awareness of labor issues within broader South Korean society. Students, intellectuals, and religious activists had long criticized the authoritarian regime on political grounds, but now such dissidents turned to workers as well and sought to link the movement for democracy to that for workers' rights.[35] Like the Russian *Narodniks* of the nineteenth century, South Korean students went to work in factories under assumed identities, risking prison and even their lives, to agitate and organize the workers. The word *minjung* (popular masses) became the general term for the broad anti-government coalition of workers, farmers, students, dissident politicians, and religious activists. This "Minjung Movement" dominated intellectual discourse in the late 1970s and 1980s.[36]

By itself, the labor movement was a major disruption to the collusive state-led development model of "Korea, Inc." Like his predecessors, President Chun tried to suppress independent labor organization, but found it impossible to do so. The number of labor disputes exploded in 1987, with nearly four thousand disputes—more than in the previous twenty-five years combined.[37] This worker unrest, alongside the large and sometimes violent student demonstrations that occurred regularly on almost every university campus from the Kwangju Incident onward—well-publicized in the Western press—created an environment of ever-growing protests that were a clear threat to Chun's authoritarian rule. To complicate matters, Seoul was to host the summer Olympics in 1988. The protests threatened to undermine Chun's attempt to use the Olympics to showcase Korea's economic achievements and his own leadership.

Chun's instinct, no doubt, was to meet these protests with violence. Unlike in Kwangju, however, this time the United States was not going to stand by and let Chun commit a massacre. In February 1987, the U.S. State Department, through Assistant Secretary of State Gaston Sigur, made it clear to the Chun government that the United States would not support a violent crackdown on the protestors.[38] In June 1987, General

Chun announced that he would step down and hold elections before the 1988 Seoul Olympics, not after as he had previously declared. Chun's announcement was followed by a presidential election in which the two major opposition figures, Kim Young Sam and Kim Dae Jung, both ran, splitting the opposition vote and essentially handing the election to Chun's chosen successor, former General Roh Tae-woo, who won the presidency with less than 37 percent of the vote. Despite its limitations, however, the 1987 elections represented a milestone in South Korea's transition to democracy, and President Roh would play an important role in laying the groundwork for future democratization.

The change of political leadership in South Korea in the late 1980s and 1990s was accompanied and promoted by new forms of civil associations and nongovernmental organizations (NGOs). Collectively, these organizations constituted an emerging civil society, engaged with and yet apart from the political system. Few countries in the world surpassed South Korea in the number, extent, and involvement of civil society groups, which often played key roles in advocating and enabling the political involvement of ordinary citizens.[39] Throughout the 1990s, South Korea witnessed the rapid growth of such associations, including environmental movements, religious organizations, organizations of students, workers, and farmers, and political watchdog groups.

By the end of the 1990s there were literally thousands of NGOs operating in South Korea. Among the more well-known activities of these groups has been the monitoring of public officials, campaigning for judicial reform and economic justice, and "disqualification" of candidates deemed unfit to run for office. Grass-roots mobilization was made even more rapid and efficient in the early 2000s through the use of the Internet, as South Korea attained one of the world's highest per capita rates of broad-band usage. "NGO" became part of almost daily South Korean vocabulary; Kyung Hee University in Seoul established what may be the only Department of NGO Studies in the world.

In December 2002 Roh Moo-hyun, a self-taught human rights lawyer and protégé of Kim Dae Jung, won the presidency over his conservative rival Lee Hoi-chang, helped in part by a highly effective, Internet-based "get out the vote" campaign among young Roh supporters. Although his margin of victory was relatively narrow, just over two percentage points, Roh's take of the total vote (48.9 percent) was higher than that of any of his three predecessors (see Table 2.1). In this sense, Roh had a stronger mandate than any previous democratically

Table 2.1   South Korean Presidential Election Results, 1987–2002

1987 Candidate (% vote)	1992 Candidate (% vote)	1997 Candidate (% vote)	2002 Candidate (% vote)
Roh Tae-woo (36.6)	Kim Young Sam (41.4)	Kim Dae Jung (40.3)	Roh Moo Hyun (48.9)
Kim Young Sam (28)	Kim Dae Jung (33.4)	Lee Hoi-chang (38.7)	Lee Hoi-chang (46.6)
Kim Jong Pil (8.1)	Chung Ju-yung (16.1)	Rhee In-je (19.2)	Kwon Yong-gil (3.9)
	Bak Ki-wan (6.3)		Lee Han-dong (0.3)
			Kim Kil-su (0.2)
			Kim Yong-kyu (0.1)

Source: Samuel S. Kim, unpublished paper, 2004. With permission.

elected South Korean president. Yet, Roh's policy directions and his sometimes provocative ways (as well as, perhaps, his status as an outsider to the political establishment) irked many of South Korea's politicians, including those in his own party, the Millennium Democratic Party (MDP).

Within a year of coming to office, Roh bolted from the MDP and formed his own party, *Yŏllin Uri Tang* or "Our Open Party" (commonly known as "Uri Party"). In March, an overwhelming majority of the National Assembly voted to impeach President Roh on charges of campaign corruption and violating the national election law. The impeachment was opposed by a substantial majority of the South Korean public, and the National Assembly elections of April 15 were widely seen as a referendum on the impeachment. If so, Roh was roundly vindicated: Roh's Uri Party won a majority of seats in the National Assembly, the conservative Grand National Party was reduced to minority status, and the MDP was trounced, falling from 59 to 9 seats in the legislature. Shortly thereafter, the Constitutional Court declared Roh's impeachment invalid, and Roh resumed the presidency.

Problems of Democracy

Despite—or perhaps because of—the depth of democratic consolidation in South Korea, a number of outstanding problems in the political system remained divisive and contentious. Among these were the underdevelopment of the political party system and the widespread public perception of cronyism and corruption among the political elites; the persistence of regional differences and divisions among the electorate; a sharp generational divide; and a re-evaluation of Korea's relations with North Korea and the United States.

If civil society was highly developed in South Korea, political society seemed still rather backward. Rather than represent any consistent ideology or platform, political parties tended to be loose coalitions of individuals centered around a leading figure or boss, and thus shifted and realigned with great fluidity. The 2004 National Assembly elections may augur a more stable two-party system, with the Uri Party and GNP representing a broad left- and right-of-center coalition, respectively[40]; but personalism and "bossism" could yet trump party discipline (Figure 2.1).

Strong regional identification in voting patterns had been a consistent element of South Korean politics since the 1960s, when Park Chung Hee began the practice of focusing economic development in, and drawing political and business elites from, his native Kyŏngsang region in the southeast, at the expense of the restive Ch'ŏlla region in the southwest (which was also the home region of Kim Dae Jung).[41] In presidential elections from 1971 onward, Kyŏngsang natives voted overwhelmingly for the candidate from their home region, Ch'ŏlla natives for theirs. Chun, also a native of Kyŏngsang, continued Park's practice of home-region favoritism. By the 2002 presidential elections, however, this regionalism had become identified with political parties. Even though Roh Moo-hyun was a native of Kyŏngsang, most Kyŏngsang voters voted for Lee Hoi-chang in 2002, while a similar proportion of voters in the southwest chose Roh. The

Figure 2.1

Migrant workers demonstrating in South Korea.

parties they represented, the Grand National Party and the Millennium Democratic Party (later the Uri Party), tended to draw their base from the Kyŏngsang and Ch'ŏlla regions respectively. In Seoul, where a quarter of South Korea's population resides, voters leaned toward Roh and the Uri Party, but often identified with their ancestral home regions. Outside Seoul, South Korean politics remained very much split along regional lines into the Roh presidency.

As more and more of the post-Korean War generation came to political maturity, the generational differences among the South Korean electorate became more pronounced. The core supporters of Roh and his party tended to come from the so-called "386" generation (people in their 30s or early 40s who went to university in the 1980s and were born the 1960s), and almost half of the National Assembly members elected in 2004 were under age 50. Compared to their elders, this generation that came of age in the democratic upheavals of the 1980s tended to be more liberal on political, social, and economic issues, less hostile to North Korea, and more independent-minded regarding South Korea's relations with the United States. The conservative supporters of the GNP, on the other hand, tended to be over age 50. The attitudes of the rising generation dominated political opinion: according to a 2004 newspaper poll, when asked their political orientation, 40.5 percent of South Koreans claimed to be "progressive," 30 percent "moderate," and only 25 percent "conservative."[42]

With the Roh-Lee presidential contest, South Korea's relations with the United States and North Korea entered into the political debate in a way that was impossible before. Previously, these relationships were simply taken for granted: the United States was South Korea's friend and patron, North Korea the enemy. But now, partly because of the rise of the younger generation to the scene, many South Koreans began to express a more complex view of both relationships. Roh Moo-hyun's promise to distance himself from U.S. policy helped his candidacy in the 2002 election, while Lee Hoi-chang's image as being too pro-American was a detriment to his. Roh's policy of engagement with North Korea had strong, though not universal, domestic support, and the relatively hard-line U.S. policy under George W. Bush was sometimes seen as an impediment to this policy. South Korea's decision to deploy troops to Iraq in 2004, though backed by Roh himself, was viewed unfavorably by many of his supporters. Few in South Korea openly questioned the necessity of a military alliance with the United States, but the relationship began to play a new role in South Korean domestic politics, and strains in U.S.-South Korean relations were much in evidence by the mid-2000s.

THE CULTURE OF "COMPRESSED MODERNITY"

The extraordinarily rapid transformation of South Korea's economy and society, at a speed and scale probably unprecedented in human history, has been dubbed "compressed modernity" by a Seoul National University sociologist.[43] In effect, the degree of socioeconomic change experienced by Europe over the course of two centuries, or by Japan in the space of sixty years, was in South Korea compressed into three decades. The cultural aspects of this compressed modernity have been less explored than the economic ones. Certainly, South Korea in the early twenty-first century could not be considered a "conservative society," if by conservative one means resistant to change. If anything, South Koreans embraced change, especially in the technological area, more than most

Western societies. Among the most striking changes were urbanization and the rise of consumerism.

South Korea in the early 1960s was a predominantly rural, agricultural society; thirty years later, it was overwhelmingly urban, with Seoul by far the largest population center in the country. Like London, Paris, or Tokyo, Seoul is the political, financial, and cultural capital as well as the nation's largest city. But to a degree greater than Britain, France, or even Japan, South Korea is a country centered on its capital. In 1949, Seoul comprised just over 7 percent of the population of South Korea; in 1990, the proportion was almost 25 percent, and in absolute numbers the city had expanded seven-fold (Table 2.2). If we include the new "satellite towns" and suburban communities whose members commute to Seoul for work, metropolitan Seoul may comprise as much as 40 percent of the population of South Korea.

With rapid industrialization and urbanization came new economic practices in everyday life, and in particular, an urban

Table 2.2 Seoul Population 1949–1990

Year	Seoul Population	% of National Population
1949	1,466,000	7.2%
1960	2,445,402	9.8%
1970	5,433,198	17.3%
1980	8,364,379	23.3%
1990	10,627,790	24.8%

Source: Adapted from Laura C. Nelson, *Measured Excess: Status, Gender, and Consumer Nationalism in South Korea* (New York: Columbia University Press, 2000), p. 36. With permission.

lifestyle oriented toward consumer comforts. South Koreans, emerging from a cultural tradition that placed a high value on frugality and disdained conspicuous consumption, for a time reacted to the rise of consumer culture with a popular backlash against "excessive consumption." Over-consumption (*kwasobi*) was commonly pointed out as one of the leading ills of South Korean society in the 1980s and early 1990s.[44] But as a high-growth economic model based on personal savings and export-oriented industry gave way to a liberalized economy focused more on domestic spending and consumption, frugality lost much of its cache. At the beginning of the twenty-first century, one of South Korea's biggest economic problems was excessive credit card debt.

These increasingly rapid changes in South Korea could be bewildering. Although South Korea remained one of the most male-dominated societies in the world in terms of political and business leadership, gender relationships were not immune to this compressed process of change. Divorce, relatively rare in the post-war period, shot up, and South Korea attained one of the highest divorce rates in the world. At the same time, birth rates plummeted; by the early 2000s South Koreans were having children below the replacement rate, and South Korea had surpassed Japan as the world's most rapidly aging society. As the society urbanized, a disproportionate number of single men remained in the countryside, and as a consequence by 2004 some 27.4 percent of rural South Korean men married foreign women.[45] Foreign workers, most from China and southern Asia but some from as far away as central Europe and West Africa, came by the hundreds of thousands to find economic opportunity in South Korea. Long considered by Koreans and foreigners alike an ethnically homogenous society,

South Korea was becoming far more ethnically diverse and multicultural than ever before in its history.

Paradoxically, while South Korea faced these cultural challenges, Korean popular culture underwent a renaissance. In the 1990s, South Korea opened up not only to American cultural imports, but also to Japanese, the latter a much more sensitive issue. The import of Japanese films, magazines, television programs, and other cultural products had been banned since the republic was founded in 1948, although a thriving illegal trade in such goods continued, in plain sight of anyone who walked past the Japanese magazine shops in the Myŏngdong commercial district of Seoul. But beginning in 1998, President Kim Dae Jung lifted the ban on such imports in stages, until by 2004 trade in cultural products carried on without any significant hindrance. Far from leading South Korea down the slippery slope to a second cultural assimilation by Japan (after the colonial assimilation policies of the 1930s), as critics of cultural opening feared, this cultural opening worked very much in South Korea's favor.

One of the most unexpected developments in South Korea's globalization at the turn of the twenty-first century has been the success of its popular culture as an export commodity. The so-called *Hallyu*, or "Korea Wave," was a term coined in South Korea to refer to the explosive growth in popularity of South Korean films, television programs, pop music, and fashions throughout Asia, especially Japan, China, Taiwan, and Vietnam.[46] Backed financially by major South Korean companies and promoted by the government, the Korea Wave found fervent, even fanatical followers in the East Asian region and beyond. Housewives from as far away as Honolulu came on group tours to visit sites filmed in their favorite Korean soap operas. Korean actors became household names in Japan. South Korean pop bands outdid the biggest American acts in popularity in China, and when visiting the country received welcomes reminiscent of The Beatles in their heyday. Vietnamese schoolgirls tried to imitate the make-up and hairstyles of their favorite South Korean singers and actresses.

Big-business underwriting and South Korean government support certainly helped raise the Korean Wave, but these alone could not explain Hallyu's success.[47] Clearly there was something about South Korean popular culture that struck a chord with young people across eastern Asia and the Pacific. This was the first time Korea had ever been a leader in cultural trends in the region, and whether the Korea Wave had staying power or was simply a flash in the pan was anybody's guess. Well into the first decade of the twenty-first century, however, Hallyu could be seen as a key element in the growing cultural integration of the East Asian region (Figure 2.2).[48]

SOUTH KOREA AS A GLOBAL POWER

Until the close of the twentieth century, Korea had never in its modern history been a major economic or political force in the East Asian region, much less the world at large. Yet despite the continued division of the Korean peninsula and the uncertain security environment in Northeast Asia, South Korea on its own has become an important country in the global economy, ranking eleventh in the world in overall national GDP. Its ships, cars, and electronics have become name-brands throughout the world; its popular culture has swept over the East Asian region and beyond; and, only a few decades removed from deep dependence on foreign aid, South Korea has established its own aid and development program

Figure 2.2
Urban Renewal, Seoul. Photo by Valerie Gelezeau, used with her permission.

for assisting Third World countries. While lacking the super-lative assets of its immediate neighbors—the population of China, the economic strength of Japan, or the military might of Russia—South Korea had achieved global clout dispropor-tionate to its relatively small size.

At its outset, the Roh administration sought to focus on South Korea's role as a key force in regional economic integra-tion, what it called Korea as the "hub economy" for Northeast Asia. In his inaugural address in February 2003, Roh said, "In this new age, our future can no longer be confined to the Korean peninsula. The Age of Northeast Asia is fast approach-ing. Northeast Asia, which used to be on the periphery of the modern world, is now emerging as a new source of energy in the global economy." Korea's position at the center for North-east Asia had long been bemoaned as the reason for Korea's weakness and victimization by stronger powers. Now, Roh declared, this very position would be Korea's advantage.

> The Korean Peninsula is located at the heart of the region. It is a big bridge linking China and Japan, the continent and the ocean. Such a geopolitical characteristic often caused pain for us in the past. Today, however, this same feature is offering us an opportunity. Indeed, it demands that we play a pivotal role in the Age of Northeast Asia in the twenty-first century.

First and foremost, Korea and the Northeast Asian region as a whole would be propelled by economic growth.

> Initially, the dawn of the Age of Northeast Asia will come from the economic field. Nations of the region will first form a "commu-nity of prosperity," and through it, contribute to the prosperity

of all humanity and, in time, should evolve into a "community of peace." For a long time, I had a dream of seeing a regional community of peace and co-prosperity in Northeast Asia like the European Union. The Age of Northeast Asia will then finally come to full fruition. I pledge to devote my whole heart and efforts to bringing about that day at the earliest possible time.[49]

The new South Korean government, in other words, sought to capitalize on its location at the center of one of the most dynamic regions in the global economy. With Japan as the world's second-largest economy, fitfully emerging from a "lost decade" of stagnation in the 1990s and in discussion for a free trade agreement with South Korea, and China, the world's fastest-growing economy and both Korea and Japan's top investment market, the three countries comprised an increasingly integrated regional economy. In the area of security, a region divided for decades by Cold War confrontation was coming together, paradoxically perhaps, over the North Korean nuclear issue, which created the opportunity for six-way security discussions involving South and North Korea, China, Japan, Russia, and the United States. For over a century, Korea had been a bystander as more powerful countries decided on the peninsula's fate. Now, with the Six-Party Talks begun in 2003 over the North Korean nuclear crisis, the two Koreas were active participants, alongside their regional neighbors and the Americans, in negotiating a peaceful outcome to the confrontation on the peninsula. The Roh government went so far as to suggest that South Korea could play the role of a mediator in disputes between Japan and China, and between North Korea and the United States. The era of Cold

War dependency, with Korea as a pawn in Great Power politics, was clearly changing.

This change was intimately connected with, and grew out of, South Korea's expanding economic power, first expressed politically in the so-called Northern Policy, or *Nordpolitik*, of president Roh Tae Woo in the late 1980s. Roh sought to use his country's economic leverage to break out of the Cold War impasse and establish political relations with communist countries in Eastern Europe and Asia, and ultimately to engage with North Korea. The strategy worked: beginning with Hungary in 1986, one East European country after another recognized the Republic of Korea. The Soviet Union itself established diplomatic relations with South Korea in 1990, and China, North Korea's closest ally, followed suit in 1992. As for North Korea, Pyongyang and Seoul signed an agreement on exchange and reconciliation in 1990 and a declaration for a nuclear-free peninsula in 1991; the two Koreas were on the verge of summit meeting when the nuclear crisis and the death of Kim Il Sung in July 1994 halted progress in North-South relations for the next several years.

Under President Kim Dae Jung, Seoul worked to cultivate good relations with all three of its major Northeast Asian neighbors, the United States, the European Union, and North Korea. With Japan, issues over Japan's militaristic past notwithstanding, South Korea engaged in active cultural exchange, trade, and tourism at levels unprecedented in the two countries' sometimes fraught relationship. Entering the new millennium, Japan and South Korea began discussions on a Free Trade Agreement. The "China boom" that South Korea had experienced since the early 1990s continued and deepened, and South Koreans put the largest share of their investment, literally and figuratively, into a rising China. Culminating Kim Dae Jung's so-called "Sunshine Policy" of engagement with North Korea, the long-delayed inter-Korean summit finally took place in Pyongyang in June 2000.

As impressive as these gains were, South Korea still faced limits to its influence and position in Northeast Asia, much less the world as a whole. Its population was far smaller than that of Russia or China, even if its economy was larger than Russia's and more advanced than China's; in any case, given China's extraordinary economic growth, reminiscent of "Korea, Inc." in its heyday but on a far larger scale, South Korea's technological lead over China was not likely to last forever. South Korea's economy was still far smaller than that of Japan and would remain so for the foreseeable future. Furthermore, as technology transfer to China accelerated, South Korea ran the risk of losing out between low-wage China and high-tech Japan. Pinning hopes on Korea as a "gateway" to China, as the Songdo Ubiquitous City project attempted to do, held no guarantee of success. As for the Korean peninsula itself, improvement of relations with North Korea, lessening the security risk of North-South tensions while avoiding an East German-style collapse of the North, which could devastate the South Korean economy, could only proceed in tandem with improved U.S.-North Korean relations. But the United States, especially under the Bush administration, took a more critical and confrontational approach to the North Korean nuclear issue than did South Korea. Seoul's ability to influence Washington's policy toward the North, given America's enormous power and different priorities, was limited.

Even with South Korea's immediate neighbors, the picture was not entirely rosy. Disputes over Japan's perceived insensitivity about its past aggression toward Korea, expressed in textbooks that downplayed Japanese atrocities in World War II and the Prime Minister's visits to the Yasukuni Shrine where numerous war criminals are interred, regularly stirred up popular outcries and government protests in South Korea, as in China. Even with China, a historical dispute over the ancient kingdom of Koguryŏ—whether it was "ethnically" Korean, as Koreans believed, or part of China, as the Chinese claimed—led to a major diplomatic row in 2004.[50]

It was in its relations with the United States that the most visible changes in South Korea's regional and global position were evident in the early 2000s. Strains in this relationship came out into the open over the U.S. troop presence in Korea, bilateral trade, the war in Iraq, and above all how to resolve the North Korean nuclear crisis. After more than a year of negotiations, all six parties to the multilateral talks over the nuclear issue agreed on a joint statement of purpose in September 2005.[51] But in reality, the goals and tactics of South Korea and the United States regarding North Korea diverged considerably. Such differences were probably inevitable, as the Cold War confrontation that created the U.S.-South Korean alliance ended both globally and, in a more subtle way, on the Korean peninsula itself. A patron-client relationship born out of the post-World War II settlement and the Korean War was evolving, sometimes painfully, into something else. Exactly what was not entirely clear. The Republic of Korea and the United States remained military allies and economic partners. But South Korea was not the destitute, peripheral, unstable regime the United States had rescued from destruction in 1950. While perhaps not yet a "whale," South Korea could no longer be called a "shrimp."

Three

North Korea: The Logic and Limits of "Self-Reliance"

During the centuries of Korea's traditional closeness to China, especially after the Ming dynasty defended Korea from the Japanese invasions of the late sixteenth century, Koreans appropriated from the Chinese philosopher Mencius the term *sadae*, "to serve the Great," to express their country's reverence for Chinese civilization and power. But in the twentieth century, with the rise of Korean nationalism, *sadae* became almost exclusively a pejorative term. *Sadae* or *sadaejùui* (Serving-the-Great-ism) was taken to mean an attitude of subservience not only to China, but to Japan, the United States, or any foreign power.[1] The antithesis of *sadae* was *chuch'e*, autonomy or independence. Although *chuch'e* was a term sometimes used in colonial Korea and in South Korea after independence as well, in the Democratic People's Republic of Korea (DPRK), *chuch'e* (*juche* in North Korean romanization) became elevated to a guiding principle of the state and an elaborate "philosophy."

From the mid-1950s to the 1990s, *juche*, often translated as "self-reliance," was a ubiquitous slogan in the DPRK, associated with cultural independence, economic self-sufficiency, national sovereignty, and the defense of the regime and its leaders.[2] More than a political or economic principle, *juche* was supposed to encapsulate a general outlook on the world, a way of life. Above all, *juche* expressed a highly nationalistic, "Korea-centric" worldview.[3] Although the term was unique to Korea, the emphasis on national self-determination expressed in the *juche* concept was common among newly independent countries and nationalist movements in the mid- to late-twentieth century. But by continuing a policy of self-reliance for decades, North Korea has become increasingly anomalous in a world characterized by deepening ties of communication and interdependence. The economic implosion of North Korea in the 1990s seemed like the inevitable result of *juche* carried to its logical and self-destructive extreme. Yet *juche*, although somewhat less emphasized since the 1990s, still occupies a central place in the official North Korean lexicon. This apparently self-defeating insistence on self-reliance, defying widespread trends toward regional and global integration, is best understood with two contexts in mind. First, *juche* is a logical, if not necessarily inevitable, product of North Korea's history. Second, *juche* is not as inflexible as North Korea's official rhetoric would suggest. North Korea has never been as self-reliant as it has claimed, and North Korea's leaders have made periodic attempts to integrate the country into both socialist and capitalist divisions of labor. By the turn of the twenty-first century, North Korea was moving slowly but decisively in the direction of greater opening, at least in the economic area. Economic self-reliance had reached its limits, but political self-determination was a nonnegotiable goal of the North Korean regime.

REGIME ORIGINS AND CONSOLIDATION, 1945–1958

Between 1945 and 1948, the northern Korean peninsula was occupied by Soviet forces, and the Red Army left a powerful imprint on the politics, economic system, culture, and world view of the nascent Democratic People's Republic of Korea. But even in the days of maximum Soviet domination, some of the peculiarities of the North Korean system could be evident to a careful observer.[4] Though a product of Stalin's Soviet Union, North Korea was never a typical Soviet "satellite" like communist Poland or East Germany, made in the Soviet image and highly dependent on Moscow for its continued existence. In its stress on nationalism, economic self-reliance, and political independence, later embodied in the concept of *juche*, North Korea in its formative years more closely resembled the neighboring, highly nationalistic communist states of China and North Vietnam than Soviet dependencies like East Germany or the Mongolian People's Republic. It is entirely possible, even likely, that North Korea would have gone in a direction largely independent of the USSR, like China or Yugoslavia, and that it might have developed into a more reform-oriented, less defensive and paranoid regime had it not been for the trauma of the Korean War and its aftermath.

The physical and human destruction of the Korean War was awesome in both North and South, but the North suffered the greater devastation. Much of this was due to the tactics and technological superiority of the United Nations forces, especially the U.S. Air Force. The United States sought to use massive and prolonged aerial bombardment as a means of breaking the morale of the North Korean population. In one two-day period the United States dropped 700 bombs on Pyongyang, which according to North Korean sources had only one building left standing at the end of the war.[5] Virtually every city in North Korea was leveled, thousands of factories were destroyed, and much of North Korea's industrial production, as well as the political leadership and population as a whole, were forced underground to avoid the bombing. The new and horrifying weapon of napalm was used on a wide scale for the first time, and at one point in the spring of 1951 the United States considered the use of atomic bombs. Finally, toward the end of the war North Korea's major dams and hydroelectric plants were bombed, creating massive flooding and destruction of food crops. Out of perhaps three million killed in the war, North Korean civilian deaths numbered more than two million, or 20 percent of the population. Millions more were injured, uprooted, or separated from their families.

Despite the war's destructiveness, the effect of the war on the regime was ambiguous. The war seems to have strengthened the position of Kim Il Sung and his partisans. Many opponents of the regime, especially Christians, fled south during the war or were executed or otherwise eliminated. The war helped to consolidate and intensify certain policies that had previously been pursued, including mass mobilization, anti-Americanism, self-reliance, and the "cult" of Kim Il Sung.[6] By April 1956, at the time of its Third Party Congress, the Korean Workers' Party claimed that membership had increased from 725,762 at the Second Congress in 1952 to a current total of 1,164,945—making the KWP, representing 12 percent of North Korea's total population, proportionately the largest Marxist-Leninist party in the world.[7]

Kim Il Sung also used the war as a means to eliminate his rivals, especially his most important rival, vice-premier and foreign ministry Pak Hŏn-yŏng. Pak had been one of the few Korean communists to survive in Korea throughout the colonial period with his well-being and political integrity intact. Pak commanded enormous respect among Korean communists, especially those from South Korea, many of whom (like Pak himself) had come north before or during the war. After the war, a dozen of Pak's allies in the political leadership were purged, put on trial as spies for the United States, and executed.[8] Pak himself was brought to trial in December 1955. His list of alleged crimes was even lengthier and more incredible than that of the twelve coconspirators, and included responsibility for the failure of a guerilla uprising in the South during the war and collusion with American soldiers, businessmen, and missionaries going as far back as 1919. Pak was given the death sentence after a one-day trial.

However, the biggest postwar leadership challenge to Kim came in 1956, shortly after the Soviet Union's "de-Stalinization" campaign began at the Twentieth Congress of the CPSU.[9] While Kim was away on a trip to the USSR and other Soviet-bloc states in June and July, a conspiracy led by pro-Chinese and pro-Soviet members of the KWP ruling circles attempted to eliminate Kim and his growing cult of personality, intending to replace him with a collective leadership. Kim scathingly attacked the conspirators at the August plenum of the KWP central committee; most leading members of this group and other accused conspirators were expelled from the party, some fleeing to China and the USSR. In a widespread purge lasting until the spring of 1958, virtually all real or potential threats to the supremacy of Kim and his partisan comrades were removed from their positions of authority, some sent into forced labor, some killed, others going into exile.[10] From then on, the core of the DPRK leadership remained a group of loyalists with close personal ties to Kim Il Sung, either through their shared Manchurian guerilla experience, or later through family connections.[11] The final purge of members of the Manchurian group itself came in the late 1960s, and there has not been any evidence of a serious political challenge to Kim from that time until his death in 1994.

Nevertheless, power struggles at the top of the political system were not reflected in political and social unrest on the part of ordinary North Koreans. After the war, the social environment in North Korea was remarkably stable, with few signs of political discontent and opposition, or indeed of crime and violence.[12] Most opponents of the regime had left during the war, and what opposition remained seems to have been eliminated by the late 1950s through improved living standards, intense ideological indoctrination, and extensive networks of surveillance and control. Most importantly, the energies of the North Korean people were channeled into the enormous project of postwar economic reconstruction (Figure 3.1).

The main processes of reconstruction were set forward by Kim Il Sung in August 1953. Priority would be given to reviving and developing heavy industry, while "simultaneously developing light industry and agriculture." This attempt at balanced growth preceded similar policies in China by several years.[13] Economic planning would advance through three stages, beginning with an initial period of preparation lasting six months

Figure 3.1
North Koreans rebuilding Pyongyang after the Korean War. From Chris
Marker, Coreénnes, Paris: Seuil, 1959, p. 54. With permission.

to one year, a Three-Year Plan to bring the economy up to pre-
war levels, and a Five-Year Plan for industrialization.[14]

By any measure, economic growth in the first decade after
the war was nothing short of astonishing. This was the period
of greatest economic success for the DPRK, not matched
before or since. The advantages of the North Korean variant
of the socialist command economy in the beginning stages of
development, including opportunities for extensive growth,
a high degree of popular mobilization, a pre-existing industrial base upon which to build, and an educated and organized
work force, put the DPRK well ahead of South Korea in economic growth until at least the mid-1960s.[15] Reconstruction
was also helped by economic aid from the USSR and other
socialist countries, amounting to $550 million according to

North Korean estimates,[16] as well as the labor and assistance of Chinese People's Volunteer troops, who remained in North Korea until October 1958.

Targets for the first Three-Year Plan (1954–56) were officially reached well before the end of three years, in August 1956; quotas for the first Five-Year Plan, launched in December 1956, were completed in 1960, one year ahead of schedule. Even if one accounts for probable exaggerations in official DPRK estimates, North Korea's economic growth in this period was one of the highest in the world. One attempt to recalculate industrial growth taking into account statistical inflation produced the following pattern:

	1949–1956	1956–1959	1960–1963
Official index (%)	9.0	45.2	15.1
Recalculated index (%)	6.6	36	7.8

Source: Joseph S. Chung, *The North Korean Economy: Structure and Development* (Stanford, CA: Hoover Institution Press, 1974), p. 76. With permission.

The estimate of 36 percent growth in the period of the first Five-Year Plan gives the DPRK a record of growth matched by few economies in modern history.

Economic development was not merely a priority in itself; development was also a means of "consolidating the democratic base" and strengthening Korean socialism. In that regard, two of the most significant goals in postwar reconstruction were the collectivization of agriculture and the appropriation of all remaining private industry by the state. Both of these goals were accomplished by 1958, completing a process of socialist transformation that had begun with the reforms of 1946.

Collectivization—or "cooperativization" (*hyŏpdonghwa*) as the North Koreans generally called it—had been enshrined as a goal in the 1948 constitution and promulgated as state policy shortly before the war, but was not put into widespread practice until after the war. As a land-to-the-tiller policy, the 1946 land reform had actually increased the number of private landowners, so that by 1953 95 percent of agricultural land in North Korea was privately owned.[17] The regime quickly set about reversing this process, bringing the entire rural population into farming cooperatives by August 1958, with 13,309 cooperatives each averaging 79 households with 134 *chongbo* of land (one chongbo being approximately 2.4 acres, or .99 ha). In October these cooperatives were amalgamated into 3,843 larger units, averaging 275 households and 456 *chongbo*. In addition, administrative districts were redrawn so that the ri or village, the lowest-level administrative unit, was identical with the cooperative farm.[18] Thus, the cooperative corresponded roughly with the "natural" village (or collection of neighboring villages) of traditional Korea, unlike large Soviet state farms. Some private farming was allowed for personal use, but in practice all farms were state-run collectives.[19]

Private ownership in industry also came to an effective end in 1958. In fact industry had been biased toward large state-run enterprises since the nationalization decree of 1946 and the first-year plan of 1947, but private business contributed significantly in a number of economic sectors as late as 1957, especially in such small-scale enterprises as food processing and metal-working.[20] In 1958 "complete socialization" of all industries was declared, and all enterprises became either state-owned operations or industrial cooperatives, with the vast majority belonging to the former category.[21] Privately-owned industry ceased to exist, signaling the "complete victory of the socialist revolution."

DEEPENING THE REVOLUTION, 1958–1972

The political and economic consolidation of the late 1950s set the basic patterns of organization, behavior, and ideology that were deepened and routinized in the 1960s, and which characterized the DPRK for the following three decades or more. These included the unassailable position of Kim Il Sung at the center of political power, surrounded by individuals linked closely to him by a common experience of anti-Japanese guerilla struggle in Manchuria or (as became increasingly important over the years) family ties; the concept of *juche*— self-identity or self-reliance—as the overarching philosophical principle guiding all areas of life, from education to foreign policy; the iconization of "Kim Il Sung Thought" (in practice indistinguishable from *juche*) as the "monolithic ideology" (*yuil sasang*) of the DPRK; the frequent use of mass mobilization and "speed campaigns" in large-scale economic projects; and a foreign policy that emphasized independence and the delegitimation of South Korea, while at the same time attempting to maintain support from both the USSR and China throughout the sometimes acrimonious Sino-Soviet split.

By the early 1970s North Korea was firmly set in all of these areas. The most important external issue remaining was reunification, which eluded the DPRK despite the political instability of South Korea in the early 1960s and North Korean attempts at assassination and subversion in the latter part of the decade. The outstanding internal issue was political succession, which was not publicly resolved until about 1980 when Kim Jong Il became heir apparent to his father, Kim Il Sung.

Ch'ŏllima, Juche, and the Cult of Kim Il Sung

By 1958, the DPRK was on a "high tide of socialist construction,"[22] and North Korea launched a new campaign that became the primary symbol of economic, political, and cultural development until the 1970s, enshrined in the DPRK constitution between 1972 and 1992.[23] The purpose of this campaign was "socialist construction," the slogan was *juche*, the technique was mass mobilization through both material and moral incentives, and the symbol was *Ch'ŏllima*, or the "Thousand-li Winged Horse." The Ch'ŏllima movement was first announced at the December 1956 plenum of the KWP Central Committee but not put into practice until 1958.[24] It bore a resemblance to both the Soviet Stakhonovite movement of the 1930s and the Chinese Great Leap Forward of the late 1950s, although the latter was declared after Ch'ŏllima and was more a coterminous influence than a direct inspiration. Workers in both agriculture and industry were exhorted to overfulfill their quotas, for which individuals would be decorated with the Order of Ch'ŏllima and particularly successful groups would be designated Ch'ŏllima Work Teams; an outstanding few received Double Ch'ŏllima awards.

The economic impact of Ch'ŏllima is difficult to assess. It certainly seems to have been less disruptive than the Great Leap Forward, which resulted in disaster and famine for millions. The North Korean economy performed well through the early 1960s, and the Five-Year Plan was declared fulfilled a year ahead of schedule in 1960. Whether or not this was the direct result of the Ch'ŏllima movement, the DPRK declared the movement a great success, and by 1961 two million workers were said to be members of Ch'ŏllima work teams.[25] One favorable assessment of the movement credits Ch'ŏllima for its balance between industry and agriculture and its emphasis on collective performance and innovation.[26]

In the early 1960s Ch'ŏllima was supplemented by two new models of economic management, both allegedly the creation of Kim Il Sung: the Chongsalli Method in agriculture and the Taean Work System in industry. Both were "mass-line" techniques that attempted to devolve decision-making to the local level and incorporate workers into the management process.[27] Economic administration was partly shifted from the central government to the county (kun), and the input of local farmers and factory workers was brought into a collective leadership system through local party committees. Cadres were sent to provincial and county work places to propagate government policies as well as elicit comments and suggestions from local workers.[28] Kim Il Sung himself was the model of this practice, regularly going to farms and factories throughout the DPRK for well-publicized "on-the-spot guidance" tours.

Kim Il Sung's first known reference to juche was in 1955, although later North Korean texts claimed the term originated in Kim's guerilla days of the 1930s. Significantly, Kim's original "juche" speech was concerned with ideological work.[29] Juche has been the preeminent expression of North Korea's emphasis on the ideological over the material, thought over matter, superstructure over base. Portrayed as a supplement to and improvement on Marxism-Leninism, juche in fact reverses the historical materialism of Marx; rather than superstructural transformation resulting from changes in relations of production, in North Korea's official ideology "thought revolution" is the first step in transforming individuals and society, out of which comes "correct" political organization, and finally increased economic production.[30] As a philosophical concept and political principle *juche* has been extremely flexible, at times nearly indefinable, but at its core *juche* reflects a deep sense of Korean nationalism and "putting Korea first."

Kim's 1955 speech emphasized the need to know Korea's unique history, geography, and culture in order "to educate our people in a way that suits them and to inspire in them an ardent love for their native place and their motherland."[31] Everyone must "have *juche*," which does not mean that individuals themselves are "self-reliant" (although the term may imply flexibility and adaptation to local circumstances), but on the contrary that individuals submerge their separate identities into the collective subjectivity of the Korean nation. In the 1960s *juche* became the key concept for an increasing range of activities, and was portrayed as an original North Korean contribution to revolutionary ideology as well as a model for other emerging Third World societies to emulate. At a speech in Indonesia in 1965, during his first official visit outside the communist bloc, Kim Il Sung declared, "*Juche* in ideology, independence in politics, self-sustenance in the economy and self-defense in national defense—this is the stand our Party has consistently adhered to."[32] In 1972 *juche* became enshrined in the DPRK constitution as the guiding principle of politics (Figure 3.2).

Figure 3.2
Juche Tower, Pyongyang. From Jan Egil Kirkebø. With permission.

North Korea in the World

After the heady years of rapid reconstruction, economic expansion, and quota overfulfillment in the 1950s and early 1960s, the North Korean economy slowed down markedly in the late 1960s. The 1961–1967 Seven-Year Plan was the first economic plan to fail to meet its deadline. In 1967 the plan was extended to 1970, becoming a *de facto* ten-year plan. Like other centralized command economies, North Korea had difficulty shifting from extensive to intensive growth and to the demands of a more complex economy, facing the common problems of bottlenecks and structural inefficiencies. Much of the spectacular economic growth of the post-Korean War years was a result of economic reconstruction and the continued movement of people from farms to factories in the early stages of industrialization. While a planned economy could be quite successful at this early stage of development, the very success of North Korea's early growth made it difficult for the DPRK to alter its policies for a more complex stage of economic development.[33] The DPRK lost outside assistance by the sharp reduction in foreign aid after 1958 and strained relations with the Soviet Union in the early 1960s. Its policy of self-reliance and hostility toward the United States, Japan, and other western countries hindered the DPRK from establishing strong economic ties to the capitalist west.

Another source of economic slowdown was the diversion of civilian resources to the military after the mid-1960s. Between 1965 and 1967 military expenditure nearly tripled, to 30 percent of total government expenditure.[34] The relative balance between heavy industry on the one hand, and light industry and consumer goods on the other, shifted markedly in favor of heavy industry and defense. Critics of this move, who advocated slower and more balanced growth, were removed from power in the last major DPRK purge of 1968–1970.[35] After 1963, the DPRK stopped releasing economic production figures.

DPRK planners, emboldened by the success of the reconstruction years after the Korean War, had overestimated the potential for economic growth in the 1960s. Nevertheless, North Korea was hardly an economic basket case by the beginning of the 1970s. Outside estimates put North Korea's GNP growth from 1961 to 1967 at a respectable 8.6 percent overall.[36] By the 1970s the DPRK had become nearly self-sufficient in energy and food, with an annual increase in grain production well ahead of population growth, according to CIA estimates.[37] Though falling behind South Korea, the DPRK's economy grew at an estimated 7.4 percent annually between 1965 and 1976, while South Korean growth approached 11 percent.[38]

A number of outside factors, including the economic rise of South Korea, the 1965 Japan-South Korean normalization treaty, and the acceleration of U.S. military involvement in Vietnam, contributed to a new mood of militarization in North Korea. Kim Il Sung spoke of the need "to turn the whole country into an impregnable fortress" to combat "American imperialism."[39] Equal weight was to be given to economic development and military preparedness. In the central government military figures rose to prominence, including Oh Chin-u, who became army chief of staff and later Defense Minister. Hostility toward South Korea shifted from rhetoric to action, indicating perhaps a North Korean attempt to emulate the North Vietnamese example of internal subversion. In 1968 several teams of North Korean guerrillas infiltrated the South, including a group of some thirty commandoes who came within a few hundred meters of the South Korean presidential palace in a failed attempt to assassinate Park Chung Hee on January 21. Two days later, on January 23, the DPRK navy seized the U.S.S. *Pueblo* off the North Korean coast, bringing tensions with the United States to their highest level since the Korean War.

Probably the most sensitive foreign policy issue in the 1960s, and continuing on until the 1980s, was North Korea's relations with China and the USSR in light of the tense—at times openly hostile—relationship between the two communist giants. During the roughly thirty years of Sino-Soviet estrangement, from the withdrawal of Soviet technicians from China in 1960 to Gorbachev's visit to Beijing in 1989, no other small communist country managed so skillfully to balance between the two. North Korea was able to maintain political, economic, and military ties with both countries throughout most of this period because of its strategic value to the USSR and China, neither of whom were willing to lose the DPRK to the other camp. For its part, North Korea insisted on an independent course: unlike Vietnam, the DPRK never joined the Soviet-dominated Council for Mutual Economic Assistance; unlike Albania, North Korea was never excommunicated from the communist bloc.

On the whole, however, North Korea has been politically and ideologically closer to China, while the Soviet Union has been more important as a military ally and source of economic assistance. Except for a period of mutual slandering and border clashes in the late 1960s, Sino-North Korean relations have been portrayed by both countries as more cordial and "fraternal," Soviet-North Korean relations somewhat cooler and more distant. China and North Korea shared a common

East Asian culture, intertwined histories, a revolutionary leadership with roots in anti-Japanese guerilla struggle, and a similar world outlook opposed to Western imperialism in general and the United States in particular. Kim Il Sung himself had spent many of his formative years on Chinese territory, fought alongside Chinese soldiers as a member of the Chinese Communist Party, and spoke Mandarin. Not least, thousands of Chinese troops had lost their lives during the Korean War, creating what the North Koreans and Chinese called a "friendship sealed in blood," a relationship "as close as lips and teeth." The USSR conspicuously had failed to make such a commitment to defending the DPRK, and the Soviet-North Korean bond was never as intimate.

When the Sino-Soviet rift first became public in 1960, North Korea attempted to remain neutral, and for a time benefited from Chinese and Soviet competition for North Korea's support. In October 1960 the USSR agreed to defer repayment of North Korean loans and offered scientific and technical assistance. In the summer of 1961 the DPRK signed treaties of "Friendship, Cooperation and Mutual Assistance" with both the USSR and China.[40] However, by 1962 North Korea showed signs of "leaning toward" China, with a concomitant decline in relations with the USSR. North Korea supported China in its border dispute with India, by then an ally of the USSR, and indirectly criticized Soviet "revisionism" and accommodation with the West (albeit in milder language than the PRC). Ch'oe Yong-gŏn, North Korea's number-two leader, visited Beijing in June 1963, for which China reciprocated by sending Liu Shaoqi to Pyongyang later that year, and the two men spoke glowingly of the friendship between the two nations. Finally, in June 1964 Pyongyang held the

Second Asian Economic Seminar, at which China and North Korea dominated the proceedings and the Soviet Union and India were visibly excluded. The event became a platform for espousing national economic self-reliance—the Chinese and North Korean model—and criticizing the USSR. The seminar was sharply attacked by the Soviets.[41]

After the fall of Khrushchev in 1964, toward whom the North Korean leadership had held mixed feelings at best since the late 1950s, Soviet-North Korean relations improved again as Sino-North Korean relations deteriorated. Soviet Premier Kosygin visited Pyongyang in February 1965, the first high-ranking Soviet official to arrive since 1961, and the DPRK's criticism of the USSR and "modern revisionism" diminished. By mid-1966, North Korea and the USSR had signed new agreements on trade and military assistance.[42] Meanwhile, China descended into the isolation and chaos of the Great Proletarian Cultural Revolution and its relations with most of the outside world, North Korea included, became militant and hostile. The PRC snubbed North Korea diplomatically at the twentieth anniversary celebrations of Korean liberation in Pyongyang in August 1945, and the Chinese press began to accuse North Korea of collusion with the "revisionists" and a lapse of revolutionary faith.[43] By the end of the 1960s Red Guard posters in Beijing labelled Kim Il Sung a "fat revisionist" and "Korea's Khrushchev"; according to Western sources, armed skirmishes occurred on the disputed Sino-North Korean border at Mt. Paektu.[44]

The late 1960s were characterized more by an alienation from China than a positive turn toward the USSR. Most of all, North Korea espoused a position of independence and wariness of "big power chauvinism," an implicit criticism of both the USSR and the PRC. The DPRK began to present itself as a model for Third World revolution and a successful example of a small nation standing up to great powers; Kim Il Sung at this time seems to have become particularly attracted to the Cuban and Vietnamese struggles against U.S. imperialism, with which the North Korean situation was expressed as having much in common.[45] North Korea in the mid-1960s also began to compete intensely with South Korea for diplomatic recognition, a subject to be taken up in Chapter 5. Toward the end of 1969 Sino-North Korea relations were on the mend, signified by Ch'oe Yong-gŏn's visit to Beijing for the twentieth anniversary celebrations of the PRC in October. Zhou Enlai visited Pyongyang in turn in April 1970, the first high-ranking Chinese official to do so since 1963. The PRC and the DPRK once again exchanged ambassadors, and relations were normalized.[46] North Korea would remain relatively balanced between, or at least never again estranged from, both China and the USSR until the end of the 1980s and the beginning of the 1990s, when first Moscow and then Beijing moved toward closer ties with South Korea over the strenuous objections of the DPRK, and the USSR itself collapsed.

TOWARD DYNASTIC SOCIALISM, 1972–1989

The problem of political succession has been acute in communist states, as in other authoritarian systems. Kim Il Sung seemed determined to avoid the struggle for power and lapse into "revisionism" that had, in his view, been so detrimental to the Soviet Union after Stalin's death. Over the course of the 1970s, while China experienced its own succession crisis with the death of Mao, Kim's eldest son Kim Jong Il was gradually built up as the leading, and finally only, candidate for succession to top leadership in the DPRK. With Kim Il Sung's death in 1994 North Korea became the only socialist state to effect a dynastic transfer of leadership from father to son.

As early as 1963 Kim Il Sung had complained of the lack of revolutionary fervor among North Korea's youth.[47] As the 1970s began Kim spoke more openly of the need for a generational transfer of power. For a time it seemed that Kim Yong-ju, younger brother of Kim Il Sung and chief DPRK negotiator for North-South talks in the early 1970s, was the leading candidate for succession. However, Kim Yong-ju's rapid ascent abruptly ended in 1975, when he was removed from the Politburo and faded into obscurity, until his sudden reemergence as vice-president shortly before Kim Il Sung's death.[48] By the late 1970s Kim Jong Il had been unquestionably designated successor to the Great Leader.

The first clear indication of Kim Jong Il's rise to prominence was his election as secretary in charge of organization, propaganda, and agitation in the Central Committee of the Korean Worker's Party in 1973. He was said to be personally directing the Three Revolution Campaigns, the DPRK's new mass mobilization movement to revolutionize ideology, technology, and culture. The Three Revolutions Campaign sent teams of twenty to fifty young party cadres to factories and farms to discuss with and guide local leaders.

In 1974 the North Korean media began to refer to a mysterious "Party Center" (tang chung'ang) said to be in charge of much of the day-to-day politics of the DPRK and second only to Kim Il Sung in power. At the Sixth Congress of the Korean Worker's Party in October 1980, this "Party Center" was revealed to be Kim Jong Il, and the younger Kim attained positions in the Secretariat, the Politburo, and the Military Commission. Only

Kim Il Sung held higher positions in all three bodies. Kim Jong Il had clearly "come out" as the number two leader in North Korea.[49]

The choice of Kim Il Sung's son as successor invoked disdain and ridicule from the DPRK's critics and less than enthusiastic endorsement from its allies. The North Koreans justified the choice of Kim Jong Il as the only candidate able to fulfill the qualities of leadership succession: youth, absolute loyalty to Kim Il Sung, thorough familiarity with Kim Il Sung's ideas, and superior intellect and ability.[50] Above all Kim Jong Il represented continuity and stability for a system increasingly threatened by events in the outside world and changes within the communist bloc.

Family succession, while a striking departure for a Marxist-Leninist state, had its precedents elsewhere in East Asia, notably Taiwan with the transfer of power from Chiang Kai-shek to Chiang Ching-kuo. It fit also into the unique North Korean fusion of a traditional Confucian stress on family background with an imported Marxist-Leninist ideology. Kim Il Sung had long said "families of revolutionaries are better in thoughts."[51] Family background affected social status, marriage prospects, and political advancement in the DPRK much as it had in Chosŏn dynasty Korea, except that the qualifications determining family background were reversed: children of revolutionaries and poor peasants were on top, descendants of landlords and colonial collaborators were on the bottom.[52] Thus, Kim Il Sung's family was the ultimate "good" family, and the logical source of political succession, according to North Korea's version of ascripted social status. In the 1980s children of other partisan fighters as well began to take positions of power in the DPRK.[53] The cult of Kim Il Sung's family was extended to include his younger brothers, uncles, grandparents, and great-grandfather Kim Ung'u, alleged to have led the "patriotic mob" that attacked the USS *General Sherman* in the Taedong River in 1866. The whole of North Korean society was thus portrayed as a family with Kim Il Sung as the benevolent father, and Kim Il Sung's family itself became the representative of North Korean society.

In the 1980s the DPRK invested a great deal of propaganda energy into portraying Kim Jong Il as brilliant, devoted, charismatic, and worthy of becoming a Great Leader in his own right. In particular Kim Jong Il was associated with culture and the arts, especially film. This may be in part a result of Kim Jong Il's personal fascination with cinema—Kim is alleged to have a private library of some 15,000 films, mostly Western— but it also reflects the primacy given to cultural production, and movies in particular, as a means of ideological indoctrination in North Korea.[54] Kim was said to have written the "definitive" book on cinematic art in 1973, and invented the "seed theory" as the conceptual basis of literature and art.[55] He was said to have produced six major films in the early 1970s, including "Sea of Blood," "True Daughter of the Party," and other North Korean "classics," and given on-the-spot guidance to the production of many others. Whatever Kim Jong Il's personal idiosyncracies, it was consistent with North Korea's stress on the primacy of "correct thought" that the political successor should begin his rise in the cultural area.

Kim Jong Il was born in Siberia during his father's retreat in the early 1940s. But in his first official biography, published in the early 1980s, Kim Jong Il was given a fictional birthplace and childhood at a "secret guerrilla camp" at the base of Mt. Paektu on the Sino-Korean border.[56] Thus the younger

Kim became associated not only with his father's guerilla background, but with the powerful image of Mt. Paektu as the sacred birthplace of the Korean people.[57] His mother Kim Chongsuk also became the object of a personality cult, and her self-sacrificing devotion to the guerilla struggle in the 1930s became the new ideal of womanhood, replacing the image of Kim Il Sung's own mother, Kang Pansŏk. By the end of the 1980s, the myth of the "Dear Leader" (ch'inaehanŭn chidoja) Kim Jong Il had nearly reached the proportions of that of the Great Leader himself.

Kim Jong Il's institutional control in North Korean politics had been consolidated over two decades by the time Kim Il Sung died. The military, which some outside observers had speculated harbored elements unhappy with Kim Jong Il, was staffed with officers having close personal ties to the younger Kim.[58] Kim Jong Il, who had no real military experience to speak of, was named Marshall of the Army in 1992, while Kim Il Sung was promoted to Generalissimo. In the party, Kim Jong Il's position has been helped by high turnover rates in the upper levels of the KWP—among the highest in the communist world—which has made career advancement highly dependent on close personal connections to Kim Il Sung and his family. Despite rumors in the West of discontent with Kim Jong Il among certain sectors of the DPRK leadership, there were few signs of any opposition to Kim Jong Il's succession after his father's death.

DECADE OF DISASTER, 1990–2000

At the beginning of the 1990s, the North Korean economy, which had encountered mounting problems since the 1960s, descended into catastrophe. Indeed, the entirety of the 1990s was a decade of disaster for the DPRK, beginning with the collapse of every communist state in Eastern Europe, proceeding to a crisis over international inspections of DPRK nuclear energy facilities that nearly led to war with the United States, the death of Kim Il Sung, and finally a series of natural calamities that pushed the North Korean food situation—never abundant to begin with—into full-scale famine.[59] North Korea spent most of the decade simply trying to cope with this compound crisis, and its leadership seemed unsure of where to take the country. Meanwhile, many in the outside world expected an inevitable collapse of the DPRK.

The threat to the DPRK's very existence in the 1990s was greater than at any time since the Korean War. North Korea's response was to batten down the hatches and proclaim its continued adherence to "socialism."[60] Pyongyang for the most part played a waiting game, maintaining the system while hoping for the "correlation of forces" to become more favorable toward the DPRK. As Paul Bracken has pointed out, the North Korean nuclear program was a way for the DPRK to "buy time for the regime to adapt to new international circumstances."[61] It is perhaps more accurate to say that the DPRK leadership wanted the world to go away until it changed more to Pyongyang's liking, but it does seem to be the case that the DPRK nuclear program was a defensive, even desperate attempt at ensuring state survival in an environment suddenly much more hostile. In this case the gamble almost backfired, as the United States and North Korea came to the brink of war in June 1994, averted at the eleventh hour by the visit of former U.S. President Carter to Pyongyang and discussions with Kim Il Sung that led, finally, to the U.S.-DPRK Framework Agreement of October 1994.

The general decline in North Korea's economic growth since the late 1950s, after a brief period of revival during the 1971–1976 Six-Year Plan, continued through the 1980s.[62] While the DPRK economy has not been as inflexible as it often appears to outsiders nor as "self-reliant" as is claimed by the North Korean government, DPRK attempts at economic reform since the 1970s have been limited and on the whole not very successful. Attempts at improving economic ties with the West, including the purchase of technology from Japan and Western Europe beginning in the early 1970s, resulted in substantial foreign debts that the DPRK was unable to repay. By 1989 North Korea had defaulted on some $5 billion in foreign debts.[63] In 1984 the DPRK established a new law allowing joint ventures with foreign companies, and in the early 1990s the DPRK established a Free Trade and Economic Zone for foreign investment in the northeast region of Najin-Sonbong.

Nevertheless, the DPRK's economic difficulties continued to worsen, reaching a point of serious crisis by the mid-1990s. North Korea's long-term structural problems were compounded by natural disasters, including severe flooding in 1995, and the loss of major sources of trade and economic assistance after the communist collapse in Eastern Europe and the USSR. Through the first half of the 1990s North Korea's economy shrank by an average 5 percent per annum, according to outside estimates, and by mid-decade its per capita GNP had fallen to one-tenth that of the South.[64]

The collapse of communist regimes in Eastern Europe and the USSR in 1989–1991 dealt a severe economic and psychological blow to the DPRK. The loss of the USSR, as the DPRK's main trading partner and superpower ally, was particularly devastating, and the absorption of East Germany by the Federal Republic of Germany appeared as an ominous portent for North Korea's future. However, contrary to expectations in the West, communism in Asia did not go the way of Eastern Europe, and the DPRK did not follow Romania and East Germany into the dustbin of history. On the contrary, the DPRK asserted that "the irreversible current of history" was still leading mankind toward socialism.[65] The DPRK, North Korea's media and leadership declared, would continue the path of *juche* regardless of events beyond its borders.

It was such an internationally isolated, impoverished, and extremely defensive DPRK that suddenly became the focus of world attention in 1991 and 1992, when the possibility emerged that North Korea was building nuclear weapons. This crisis, to be explored in more detail in Chapter 5, brought the United States and North Korea closer to war than at any time since the *Pueblo* incident of January 1968. At the peak of the confrontation, in June 1994, a full-blown catastrophe was averted by the intervention of former U.S. President Jimmy Carter, who met with Kim Il Sung in Pyongyang to discuss direct U.S.-North Korean talks on the nuclear issue. On June 22, U.S. President Bill Clinton agreed to negotiate with North Korea over the possibility of trade and diplomatic ties between the two countries in exchange for North Korea suspending its nuclear activities.

On July 8, 1994, the day the negotiations were set to begin in Geneva, Kim Il Sung suddenly died. The whole of North Korean society went into a paroxysm of grief over the loss of the only leader they had ever known, a man who had virtually become a deity. Yet the chaos and uncertainty of political transition long anticipated by the West did not come about. After a suitable period of mourning Kim Jong Il appeared to take charge, a major leadership struggle did not take place, and the DPRK continued negotiations over nuclear inspection.

A U.S.-DPRK "Framework Agreement" to resolve the nuclear issue was signed by U.S. Assistant Secretary of State Robert Gallucci and North Korean Vice-Foreign Ministry Kang Sŏkju on October 21, 1994. The agreement stipulated a strict set of quids pro quo: over a ten-year period, North Korea was to dismantle its existing nuclear facilities and ship out spent fuel rods to third countries for disposal, adhere to IAEA safeguards, and open all nuclear facilities for inspection. In exchange, the United States was to lead a consortium called the Korea Energy Development Organization (KEDO), including South Korea and Japan, to build two light-water nuclear reactors in North Korea supplying 2,000 megawatts of power at a cost of some $4 billion. In the interim the United States would supply heavy oil to meet North Korea's energy needs, up to 500,000 tons per year. Meanwhile, the United States and DPRK would work toward establishing liaison offices in each other's capitals, and the United States pledged not to threaten North Korea with nuclear weapons while the DPRK remained a member in good standing of NPT.[66]

The nuclear issue did not end with the Framework Agreement, but it was a major step toward resolution. North Korea had been offered a free supply of desperately needed energy, and equally important had finally opened up the possibility of economic assistance and diplomatic recognition from the United States. The DPRK's high-stakes game of playing on the outside world's uncertainty over its nuclear program had brought about substantial pay-offs. At the risk of international pariah status and possibly military attack, North Korea had won a breathing space for the continuity of the regime. The continued existence of the Democratic People's Republic, despite economic crisis, leadership transition, and an increasingly hostile international environment, was in itself no small achievement.

A TENTATIVE TURN OUTWARD

By the beginning of the new millennium North Korea emerged from its preoccupation with sheer survival and began to turn outward toward improving relations with Western countries, Russia, and South Korea. Although North Korea's economic problems were far from resolved, the imminent collapse of the DPRK regime itself seems to have been, if not eliminated as a near-term possibility, at least postponed for the immediate future. With the possible exception of the United States, most of the world seems now to accept the premise that the DPRK is a viable state that must be dealt with as it is, and any positive change will more likely come about through engagement rather than isolation. This is the logic behind Kim Dae Jung's much-criticized "Sunshine Policy" of engagement with the North. For its part, North Korea after the end of the 1990s, and with the encouragement of South Korea, became increasingly connected to the outside world through new diplomatic ties, economic exchange, and membership in multilateral organizations.

While a new nuclear confrontation between the United States and North Korea broke out in October 2002, on the Korean peninsula itself, the trajectory was almost exactly the opposite of the increasingly hostile U.S.-North Korean relationship. North-South relations in the new millennium had never been better, as exemplified above all by the Kim Jong Il-Kim Dae Jung summit in Pyongyang in June 2000. To be sure, the high hopes of the June 2000 summit went largely unfulfilled. Kim Jong Il never made the reciprocal visit to South Korea promised at the time of the summit, which caused no small embarrassment for and opposition criticism of Kim Dae Jung. The inter-Korean railways and roads were officially reopened, but little traffic flowed on them. The South Korean tours to the Kumgang Mountains in eastern North Korea, sponsored by the Hyundai conglomerate, turned out to be a major money-losing venture. Nevertheless, the symbolic value of the North-South summit was enormous, if only for signaling that North Korea was rejoining the wider world. Beginning with the normalization of ties with Italy in January 2000, North Korea launched an unprecedented diplomatic courtship of western countries. Within two years, Pyongyang had established diplomatic relations with all but two of the European Union member states, the EU itself, Canada, Australia, the Philippines, Brazil, and New Zealand. In July 2000, with Seoul's encouragement, North Korea joined the ASEAN Regional Forum for intra-Asian security dialogue. North Korea also attempted to mend fences with Russia, and Kim Jong Il visited both China and Russia in 2001, his first official visits abroad as North Korean leader. After a decade of inward-looking crisis management and confusion, North Korea—with South Korea's help and encouragement—had made a significant turn outward.

In terms of economic life, there were some indications of change—and even the use of the heretofore taboo word "reform"—in both the rhetoric and the observable reality of DPRK life. Since the economic crisis began to emerge in the early 1990s, long before the famine, there had been signs of liberalization and the growth of local markets in the North Korean economy, what one American observer calls "reform by stealth."[67] In January 2001 the *Rodong Sinmun* announced a policy of "New Thinking" (*Saeroun kwanjom*), which called for scrapping outmoded habits and mentalities and putting all efforts into the technological reconstruction of North Korea.[68]

The very phrase "New Thinking" was strikingly reminiscent of former Soviet leader Gorbachev's *perestroika* (restructuring), and in the North Korean case the term emphasized ideological and economic flexibility, industrial restructuring, and a focus on computers and information technology.[69] In order to accomplish this, the DPRK demonstrated a new willingness to learn from the outside world. In 2001, for example, North Korea sent nearly 500 government officials and students abroad to study technical subjects, economics, and business, mostly in other Asian countries and in Australia—almost triple the number Pyongyang had sent in 2000.[70] There were even a small number of North Korean students studying, with little fanfare or publicity, in the United States.

Despite heightened tensions with the United States, North Korea continued on the path of internal reform. A year after "New Thinking" was officially launched in January 2001, the 2002 New Year's Joint Editorial in the three main official DPRK newspapers celebrated the "successes" of the previous year and renewed the call for "radical change" in the economy.[71] In March 2002, the Supreme People's Assembly, North Korea's highest legislative body, approved a budget emphasizing technical innovation and modernization.[72] The second half of 2002 saw some of the boldest steps yet toward real reform in the DPRK. At the beginning of July 2002, the DPRK had begun to institute some of the most far-reaching economic changes since the regime was founded in 1948. The food distribution system on which much of the population had depended (at least until the famine of the 1990s) was reduced and modified; the price of rice was raised to near-market levels, and wages were correspondingly increased as much as thirty-fold; the official exchange rate for the North Korean *won* was reduced from 2.2 to nearly 200 to the dollar, approaching the black market rate; and the taxation system, abolished in 1974, was reportedly revived.[73]

The results of this economic restructuring were mixed. Foreign companies did not flock to North Korea as Pyongyang's leaders may have hoped. A model Special Economic Zone (SEZ) established in the city of Sinŭiju on the Sino-North Korean border failed to take off when Chinese authorities arrested the man personally appointed by Kim Jong Il to run the SEZ, a wealthy Chinese native of Dutch citizenship named Yang Bin, before he could start the project.[74] North Korea was beset by inflation, and while senior party officials and other elites with access to foreign exchange could cope with the changes, many ordinary North Koreans were adversely affected by the rise in food prices.[75] But the DPRK government did not retract the July 2002 reforms and continued to call for restructuring. It even attempted to revive the Sinŭiju SEZ project under an appointed leader even more unlikely than Yang Bin: Julie Rixiang Sa, a Korean-born, ethnic Chinese U.S. citizen, and former (Republican) mayor of Fullerton, California.[76] At the same time, the DPRK started to announce a new "Military-First Politics" and the need for stronger defense against "imperialism." These moves can be interpreted as a reaction to changed external circumstances, above all a U.S. administration perceived as more dangerously hostile to North Korea's existence as well as a defense of the military's domestic interests in a new age of North Korean *perestroika*. The 2003 New Year's Joint Editorial combined militaristic rhetoric with renewed calls for change in the economy and repeated the earlier slogan of "ensuring the greatest profitability while firmly adhering to socialist principles."[77] The DPRK seemed determined to continue with economic reform under the firm control of the party-military apparatus, perhaps even moving toward a military-led modernizing state somewhat along the lines of South Korea in the 1960s and 1970s.[78] This could all be too little, too late to save the North Korean regime. But for well over a decade, since the collapse of the East European communist regimes and the Soviet Union, North Korea had defied predictions of its imminent demise. As much as the DPRK appears to be an aberration in the twenty-first century, the world may have to learn to live with North Korea for some time to come.

Four

The Korean Diaspora

The large-scale movement of people outside their place of origin, whether voluntary or forced, is very much part of the modern condition. It is also an integral part of Korea's collision with modernity. The emergence of large communities of Koreans residing outside Korea proper is almost exactly coterminous with the period of modern globalization, from about 1860 to 1945. It was a period of political confusion, economic transformation, imperial aggression, colonization, and war. Chosŏn Korea before the upheavals of the late nineteenth century was not hermetically sealed, as critics of the "Hermit Kingdom" might suggest, but the kingdom did place severe restrictions on movement in and out of the peninsula. No significant, self-identified community of Koreans existed outside the Korean peninsula before the second half of the nineteenth century. At the end of World War II, some 11 percent of the population of Korea resided outside the peninsula,[1] and communities of hundreds of thousands of ethnic Koreans resided in three foreign countries: Japan, China, and the Soviet Union. A fourth Korean community, that of the United States, was much smaller than the first three until after the mid-1960s, but from that point onward it grew rapidly, until by the turn of the millennium, Korean Americans had become the largest overseas Korean group. Smaller numbers of Korean immigrants and their descendants live also in Canada, Western Europe, Latin America, and elsewhere in the Asia-Pacific.

Whether we can call this a diaspora, as some now do, is debatable. The term "diaspora," most often associated with the Jews, suggests forced removal from the homeland and oppression in the host country that do not apply to many of the Koreans overseas (although in some cases, they do apply). In recent years, "diaspora" has come to be applied to any widely dispersed, self-conscious ethnic community separated from its country or region of ancestry—Africans, Armenians, Chinese, Indians, and so on.[2] In the sense of wide dispersal and ethnic self-consciousness, we may see the overseas Korean communities as a diaspora, broadly defined. But the degree of self-identification as "Korean" varies considerably across geography and generation, despite the attempts of each of the two contemporary Korean states to identify all people of Korean ancestry unproblematically as "overseas Koreans."[3] The Overseas Korean Foundation in South Korea, for example, lists the statistics shown in Table 4.1.

It is not clear from Table 4.1 how these statistics were gathered, how one is defined as "Korean," or whether or not the people listed in these figures necessarily saw themselves as "overseas Koreans." As with other diasporas, the degree of Korean identification with the "homeland" varies according to

Table 4.1 Koreans residing outside the Korean Peninsula

Country	Number of Korean Residents
U.S.A.	2,123,167
China	1,887,558
Japan	640,234
Commonwealth of Independent States (former Soviet Union)	521,694
Canada	140,896
Brazil	48,097
Australia	47,227
Germany	30,492
Argentina	25,070
Philippines	24,618
Mexico	19,500
Indonesia	18,879
New Zealand	18,338
Britain	15,000
France	10,485
Thailand	9,870
Vietnam	6,226
Paraguay	6,190
Guatemala	6,190
Singapore	5,456
Italy	4,960
Taiwan	2,945
Malaysia	2,937
Nations with a Korean population of under 2,000	35,765
Total (151 countries)	5,653,809

Source: Overseas Koreans Foundation. http://okf.or.kr/eng/index.html.

the community and the individual. A further peculiarity of the Korean case is that there are, in effect, two homelands: North Korea and South Korea. Therefore, the relationship between a particular diasporic Korean community and the government of the "home" country is rarely straightforward. Diaspora has sometimes been called the "other" of the nation-state, and a diasporic community almost always refers in some way back to a nation-state—whether currently existing, historical, or imagined.[4] For Koreans, both the diasporic condition and the modern nation-state itself are highly problematic, and while both Korean states make claims to the loyalty of Koreans abroad (as well as Koreans living under the other Korean state), the reality is division in the homeland and dispersal abroad. Division and diaspora are two of the defining characteristics of contemporary Korea.

Whether or not one accepts at face value the numbers of overseas Koreans cited by Korean governments, such figures do give a reasonably accurate sense of the proportions of people with Korean ancestry in different geographical areas. Modern Korean migration began first as a movement across the northern boundaries of the peninsula to China and Russia in the late nineteenth century, then eastward to Japan and the United States in the twentieth century. These four areas today (including the states of the former USSR) host the vast majority of the Korean diaspora, or about five of the estimated six million overseas Koreans. As it happens, the four largest overseas Korean communities offer a unique test case of ethnic adaptation and community development in four different types of nation-states: allegedly mono-ethnic Japan, officially multinational China, the ostensibly multicultural United States, and the new republics of the former Soviet Union.

DIASPORA BEFORE DIVISION
Continental Migration, 1860–1945

Modern Korean emigration coincides with the global rise of mass long-distance migration in the second half of the nineteenth century, a process that reached its peak in the 1920s and 1930s. The stereotypical emigrant of the time, at least in the Western imagination, is a peasant from Eastern or Southern Europe boarding a ship for America. This type of emigration, while important, is just part of the total picture. As the historian Adam McKeown has pointed out, there were in fact three major routes of long-distance migration in this period, each of approximately equal size (50–60 million): across the Atlantic from Europe to the Americas; from India and southern China to Southeast Asia, the Indian Ocean rim, and the South Pacific; and by land from Northeast Asia (including northern China, the Korean peninsula, and Russia) to Manchuria, Siberia, Central Asia, and Japan.[5] Before the twentieth century, when Koreans began settling across the Pacific, Korean migration was part of this third route, which is the least studied of the three.

Several factors contributed to the rise of Korean emigration from the early 1860s onward. First, partly to offset the growing Russian encroachment into Northeast China, the Qing government relaxed its restrictions on Chinese migration into the region, also known as Manchuria. The Koreans were indirect beneficiaries of these relaxed migration policies, especially after Qing officially opened migration into Manchuria for non-Chinese in the 1880s. Second, the Russian empire annexed part of the Pacific coast from China in 1860, giving Russia for the first time a border with Korea, an eleven-mile strip along the Tumen River. This border was poorly policed and Koreans could cross into Russia with relative ease. Third, within Korea, economic hardship, famine, and related social discontent in the northern areas motivated many Korean farmers to leave their country for economic opportunities abroad. Finally, the Chosŏn government itself, faced with internal difficulties and pressures from Russia and China, relaxed its restrictions on cross-border movement. The last two decades of the nineteenth century were also the period when, for the first time, a significant immigrant community settled in Chosŏn: Chinese migrants, mostly from across the Yellow Sea in Shandong Province, who established Chinatowns in Inch'ŏn, Seoul, and other Korean cities.

Of course, people had moved across the borders between Korea and its Northeast Asian neighbors for millennia, even if, for much of that time, such movement had been more restricted than it was in the late nineteenth and early twentieth centuries (and would become restricted again after the establishment of post-war boundaries in the 1940s and 1950s). The novelty of this emigration from Korea lies not merely in its size and speed of growth. The new migration coincided with the rise of modern nationalism, although the relationship between the two was complex and sometimes contradictory. On the one hand, relatively large and self-contained communities of Korean migrants, especially in Northeast China and Pacific Russia, maintained the language, many of the cultural practices, and arguably a sense of cultural identity from their Korean homeland (at least among the first generation). On the other hand, the Chosŏn government had little if any authority over its former residents abroad, and the connection between the emigrant communities and the Korean state as such was usually weak and tenuous. We can say then there may have been a sense of "ethnic" or cultural identity in these early Korean immigrant communities, but probably little identification with the Korean nation-state. After Japanese annexation in 1910, Russia, Manchuria, and China proper became the destinations of a growing number of nationalist-oriented intellectuals and political activists. These migrant communities thus became sites of new, contested visions of a modern independent Korea. The politics of postliberation Korea would, to a considerable extent, be led by former exiles returning from China, Russia, and the United States.

Korean emigration into China was concentrated in the area just across the Tumen River from Korea, first known as Jiandao in Chinese and Kando in Korean, and later officially called Yanbian (Chinese) or Yŏnbyŏn (Korean) after the establishment of the People's Republic of China in 1949 (although the name Yanbian had also been in use earlier). The region is now the Yanbian Korean Nationality Autonomous Prefecture of China's Jilin Province. Initially most of the Korean settlers were from the Hamgyŏng provinces of the far north of Korea, although later groups came from the P'yŏngan region as well as southern Korea.[6] By 1910, some 220,000 Koreans lived in Jiandao; by 1931 Koreans in the area numbered over 900,000, three times as many as the local Chinese.[7] After Japan declared Korea a protectorate in 1905, the Japanese authorities attempted to penetrate the Jiandao region, using Korean residents as a pretext to establish a police presence there.[8] Colonization accelerated the process of Korean migration. Koreans after 1910 were ostensibly Japanese subjects, albeit second-class subjects within the empire, and the Japanese government and military encouraged Korean migration as a means of extending Japanese interests in the region. After the pro-Japanese state of Manchukuo was carved out of Northeast China in 1932, Japanese themselves were also encouraged to migrate en masse to Manchuria, although the official goal of nine million Japanese farmers in Manchuria was never realized.[9] Whatever their views of the Japanese presence in the region—which was ambivalent at best—Koreans continued to migrate into Manchuria throughout the colonial period. At the end of World War II, nearly two million Koreans lived in Northeast China, the second-largest group of Koreans outside the peninsula, next to the Korean community in Japan. By then many Koreans in China had become permanent settlers, and only about half returned to Korea after liberation.

China became the haven for the largest number of Korea's pro-independence political activists after the March First Independence Movement in 1919. The Provisional Government of the Republic of Korea (KPG) was established in Shanghai in April 1919; its leaders included Syngman Rhee, who soon left the Provisional Government for his own organization in the United States, and Kim Ku, the most prominent right-wing nationalist of the colonial period. Yi Tong-hwi, who founded the Korean People's Socialist Party in Vladivostok in 1918, renamed his organization the Korean Communist Party and joined forces with the Shanghai group as well. In addition, Korean nationalists formed a Korean Restoration Army (Chosŏn Kwangbokkun) in Manchuria. Relations between communists and nationalists among the Korean political exiles were often rocky, and many of the Korean communists in China—with Moscow's encouragement—joined the Chinese Communist Party in the late 1920s and 1930s. The leading Korean communist groups in China were the groups aligned with Mao in

China proper, later called the Yanan Group after Mao's Chinese Communist Party wartime redoubt; and the members of the multi-ethnic Northeast Anti-Japanese United Army in Manchuria, which included future North Korean leader Kim Il Sung. After the Japanese attacked Shanghai in 1937, the Korean Provisional Government fled with Chiang Kai-shek's nationalist Guomindang to Chongqing, in the Chinese interior. Unlike the Guomindang, however, the KPG was never recognized by the United States or other Western allies as the legitimate government of Korea.

In Russia, as in China, most of the early Korean settlers came from the nearby border regions of northern Korea. The first recorded migration occurred in 1863, when thirteen Korean families crossed the Tumen River into the Russian Maritime Region. By 1885, 3,000 Koreans were arriving annually, and by the time of the Bolshevik Revolution in 1917, 100,000 Koreans resided in the region, comprising some 30 percent of the total population.[10] The Koreans' relationship to the Russian (later Soviet) state was complex, as were the Russians' attitudes toward and treatment of the Korean immigrants. In 1888 the Czarist government offered the Koreans citizenship, and by 1902 about half had taken up the offer. The early Korean immigrants tended to be farmers, perceived as hardworking and generally loyal to the Russian authorities. Initially, the Russian government welcomed Korean settlers to help in the cultivation and colonization of the Russian Far East. But Russian attitudes toward Koreans were also influenced by racist fears of a "Yellow Peril" that allegedly threatened European Russians' dominant position in the Far East. It was in this context that Koreans became victims of Russian fear of the Chinese, and then—quite ironically—of the Japanese.

After 1910 Russia, like China, became a haven for Korean nationalists fleeing Japanese persecution. The 1917 revolution, with its official anticolonial stance, inspired Korean nationalists both in Korea and abroad. Many Koreans in Russia joined the Bolshevik side in the Russian civil war, and the first socialist-oriented Korean political party was formed in the Russian Far East in 1918. The Korean communist movement was born on Russian soil among Korean exiles.[11] But advocating Korean independence was one thing, self-determination of Koreans within Russia quite another. By the 1930s, tensions between the USSR and Japan mixed with Russian racism and Stalinist terror to create an explosive mix, with grievous consequences for the now-Soviet Koreans. In the mid-1930s, ethnic Chinese and Korean members of the Communist Party of the Soviet Union were expelled from local party branches in the Russian Far East. Most extraordinarily of all, the Soviet government used the argument of ethnic Koreans being spies for Japan—despite the clear record of anti-Japanese political activities among the Koreans in Russia—as a pretext to deport almost the entire community of Koreans, which numbered some 200,000 by this time, from the Soviet Far East to Central Asia. The Koreans were one of the first minority groups in the USSR to undergo forced deportation, a process that ultimately moved millions of people willy-nilly around the Soviet Union—Germans to Kazakhstan, Poles to Siberia, Finns to Central Asia, Jews to the Far East, Ukrainians, and so on.[12] In the fall of 1937, at least 175,000 Koreans (possibly many more) were taken by train to Central Asia, mostly Kazakhstan and Uzbekistan.[13] There the deportees, migrants for a second time, tried to survive in a climate and physical and cultural environment drastically different from what they had grown accustomed to in the Russian Far East. Some turned to farming, albeit primarily cotton farming rather than the rice farming they were used to, but over time the majority settled in cities, making Almaty (Kazakhstan) and Tashkent (Uzbekistan) the largest Korean population centers in the Soviet Union.

Migration into Japan

Modern Korean emigration to Japan began somewhat later than continental migration to China and Russia, and throughout the twentieth century, the Korean community in Japan has had arguably the most difficult time of any overseas Korean community. Koreans and Japanese, across the body of water that separates their two countries but especially within their own countries, have tended to view each other with suspicion, distrust, and dislike far more than with any positive feelings. Koreans today constitute the only significant ethnic minority within Japan, and among the four largest settlements of Koreans overseas—in China, the former USSR, the United States, and Japan—only in Japan have Koreans consistently, up to the present, maintained the status of an underclass.

Although Korea and Japan entered into modern diplomatic relations in 1876, thanks to Japan's successful gunboat diplomacy at Kangwha Island, Koreans did not migrate to Japan in any significant numbers until the twentieth century. If anything, the movement was in the other direction, with Japanese farmers, businessmen, and government and military officials going to Korea. However, for a small group of reform-minded Korean intellectuals in the late nineteenth century, men of the elite classes such as Kim Ok-kyun, Pak Yŏng-hyo, and Yun Ch'i-ho, Meiji Japan offered an attractive model for Korea's own modernization.[14] To such Koreans Japan represented "the West"—or more precisely, the only successful example of independent "Westernization" in Asia—and a number of Koreans traveled to Japan to study Japan's lessons for Korea, some working under the renowned liberal scholar Fukuzawa Yukichi. But Japan-as-model soon became Japan-as-conqueror, and by the time of Korea's March First Independence Movement in 1919, the very students who had gone to study Japan's modernization had taken the lead in the struggle against Japanese domination.

Nevertheless, the number of Korean students and other immigrants in Japan continued to grow in the relatively liberal 1920s, the time of "Taisho democracy" in Japan and "cultural rule" in Korea. The influx of this new immigrant population created new tensions and anxieties within Japanese society, which came to a head in 1923. On September 1 that year, a massive earthquake centered on the Kanto plain shook the main Japanese island of Honshu, killing between 100,000 and 200,000 people. In the resulting chaos, a rumor spread that Koreans were poisoning wells and killing innocent Japanese. This led to violent attacks against Koreans, along the lines of a classic European anti-Semitic pogrom; at least 6,000 Koreans were murdered, and many more injured or imprisoned.[15] The Japanese police, military, and local government did little if anything to prevent the violence, and even helped to promote it. The modern Korean immigrant community in Japan had gotten off to a very poor start.

At the end of the 1920s and into the 1930s, the Korean population in Japan began to be transformed from a largely male community of students to a more mixed-gender community of long-term residents. In 1925 the male-female ratio of Koreans in Japan was seven to one; by 1939 it was 1.5 to one.[16] The immigration rate declined during the Depression years, then shot up during the wartime mobilization of the late 1930s. The war against China that began in 1937, and against the United States in 1941, created a labor shortage in Japan, one that the government chose to fill largely with workers from the Korean colony. The Labor Mobilization Law of August 1939 brought hundreds of thousands of Koreans to work in the mines and factories of Japan, as well as the mines of southern Sakhalin, a coal-rich area taken from Russia in 1905, after the Russo-Japanese War.

Korean workers were brought in to replace Japanese men drafted for war. At the beginning, Koreans were not trusted to join the Japanese military, although they were allowed to join on a voluntary basis from 1938 onward, and were finally conscripted after 1942. A select few attended Japanese military academies, including future South Korean President Park Chung Hee, who graduated from the Manchurian Military Academy in 1944. Altogether over 100,000 Koreans participated in the Japanese wartime military, most as low-ranking draftees. Koreans gained particular notoriety as prison guards for Allied POWs in Southeast Asia.[17] Most notoriously of all, tens of thousands of Korean women and girls were drafted as sexual slaves, the so-called "Comfort Women," by the Japanese Imperial Army.[18] The Pacific War was a brutal experience for Japan as a whole. For most Koreans, second-class subjects of empire both in Korea and in Japan, the war was a trauma of ethnic discrimination and forced labor. When Japan surrendered to the Allies in August 1945, some 2.4 million Koreans lived in Japan.[19] Most wanted to return to Korea, and many Japanese were quite happy to see them leave.

Trans-Pacific Migration

Korean emigration to the United States has been almost entirely a twentieth-century phenomenon. A few Koreans went to the United States to study in the 1880s and 1890s. Yu Kil-chun, a pioneering Christian reformer, has the distinction of being the first Korean to do so, at the Governor Drummer Academy in Massachusetts. His contemporary Sŏ Chae-p'il (Philip Jaisohn) was the first Korean to become an American citizen and the first to obtain an American medical degree, from the University of Pennsylvania in 1892. Sŏ returned to Korea in 1896 to become a leader of the reform movement, and although he was to reside in the United States for many years, like most other Korean students of the time Sŏ had not intended to make the United States his home. Except for a few dozen scattered students, diplomats, and workers, no Korean "community" as such existed in American territory until 1903, when Koreans were brought to work in the sugar cane fields of Hawaii.[20] By the end of 1905 over 7,000 Koreans had settled in Hawaii, the vast majority single men, working grueling hours for menial pay in the tropical sun. Between 1910 and 1924, Korean "picture brides" were allowed to immigrate to the United States to join their prospective husbands in arranged marriages. As the term "picture bride" suggests, such women were usually acquainted with their husbands-to-be only through photographs sent to them in Korea from Hawaii. Japanese immigrants in Hawaii also followed this practice; needless to say, the men they met in Hawaii often failed to meet the expectations raised by the photographs.

The U.S. government put a stop to labor and "picture bride" immigration with the 1924 Immigration Act, which excluded nearly all immigration from Asia. From then until the Korean War, Korean emigration to the United States virtually ceased. Gradually, the Korean community within the United States expanded from Hawaii to the mainland, especially southern California, and Los Angeles eventually supplanted Honolulu as the center of the Korean community in the United States, a position it still retains today. One of the first Koreans born on the U.S. mainland was Philip Ahn, born in 1905 in Los Angeles, who was the son of the prominent Korean independence fighter An Ch'ang-ho. The younger Ahn became famous in his own right as a film and television actor, mostly playing stereotypical Asiatics for Hollywod. Ahn's best-known role was that of Master Kan in the 1970s television series "Kung Fu." Even so, in the 1930s there were still only 650 Koreans in Los Angeles, a tiny fraction of the size of the Japanese- and Chinese-American communities in the area, and as late as 1970 Los Angeles County contained only 8,900 Koreans, comprising 13 percent of the Korean American population as a whole.[21] Two decades later, there would be at least twenty times as many Koreans in Southern California alone, with hundreds of thousands more in other parts of the United States.[22]

After 1910, Koreans were officially treated as Japanese subjects by the U.S. government, and even as early as the Japanese Protectorate period (1905–1910) the United States only recognized Koreans with passports issued by Japan. This created a paradox after Pearl Harbor—whereas the Korean community in the United States was largely pro-independence, Koreans as Japanese subjects should have been considered enemy aliens. Nevertheless, unlike Japanese-Americans, Koreans in the United States were not sent to internment camps.

U.S. Military Order No. 45, promulgated in December 1943, exempted Koreans from enemy alien status.

By 1945 the Korean immigrant population in the United States numbered only a few thousand, a miniscule population compared to the ethnic Korean communities in Japan, China, and Russia, and far smaller than the population of Americans of Chinese or Japanese descent. Nevertheless, the United States had been a haven for some of the most prominent pro-independence leaders, including Sŏ Chae-p'il, An Ch'ang-ho, and Syngman Rhee. Rhee in particular held tenaciously to the hope that the United States would defeat Japan and bring freedom and self-determination to Korea, preferably under Rhee's own leadership. He shuttled between lobbying the State Department and other government agencies in Washington for the cause of Korean independence, and raising funds and support among the Koreans in Hawaii. Rhee's lobbying was not entirely successful, as the United States refused to put its full weight behind Rhee until 1947, and even then did so rather reluctantly. As exemplified by Rhee's experience, the Korean independence movement in the United States was quite different in character than that of Russia, China, or Japan. In the United States, there was no large independent political organization of Koreans, no government-in-exile, or ethnic Korean guerilla army. In America, the Korean independence movement was led by highly educated, often elitist men such as Rhee. In particular, there was no organized left-wing party in the United States that was instrumental in mobilizing the Korean independence movement as was the Communist Party in China, Japan, and the Soviet Union. Like the Korean-American community as a whole, indeed like the United States as a whole, the Korean independence movement in America was predominantly

Christian, urban, and liberal. Rhee and other American-educated Koreans played a critical role in fashioning a pro-U.S. South Korea after independence, but represented only one part of a much larger political spectrum.[23]

"OVERSEAS COMPATRIOTS" AND THE TWO KOREAN STATES

From the time of their founding, each of the two Korean states claimed to speak for the entire Korean people, which meant not only Koreans on the peninsula, but "compatriots" abroad as well. Part of the intense competition between the two Koreas has been for the recognition and support of Koreans overseas. In the early post-Korean War decades, the North Korean government put relatively more resources into cultivating the support of the overseas Koreans, especially in China and Japan. South Korea paid less attention to Koreans abroad until around the 1970s; since then, the change in relative economic position and international status between the two Koreas has meant that, on the whole, South Korea has become more successful than the North in its acceptance as the legitimate Korean "motherland" by Koreans overseas. But there are exceptions to this, most notably among Koreans in Japan, as well as a general trend among ethnic Koreans abroad in recent decades to identify more with their country of residence than with either Korean state.

In both North and South Korea, the official term for Koreans abroad is "Overseas Compatriots" (*Haeoe tongp'o*). At least informally, people of Korean descent living outside the Korean peninsula, regardless of citizenship, are considered "Korean." In the DPRK, overseas compatriots visiting the country have a status distinct from that of "ordinary" foreigners and are dealt with through a special government agency. In South Korea, the special status of "overseas Koreans" is less formalized, but there has been a strong perception of ethnic consanguinity between Koreans in Korea and compatriots abroad. At the same time, Koreans who adopt foreign citizenship automatically renounce ROK citizenship, and retrieving South Korean citizenship is difficult. Attempts on the part of the South Korean legislature to allow dual citizenship for overseas Koreans have been unsuccessful, not least because of fears in South Korea that this would open the door for thousands of unwanted, impoverished "compatriots" from China and the former Soviet Union to enter the ROK. Before the late 1980s, the migration of ethnic Koreans from current and former communist countries was not possible. With the rise of an affluent South Korea and the erosion of Cold War barriers to movement in Northeast Asia, such compatriots are no longer a mere abstraction, but real people visiting and working (often illegally) in South Korea. South Koreans themselves were not able to travel abroad freely until the 1990s. In the last two decades, more extensive and sustained contact between Koreans in the South and Koreans outside the peninsula—and, most recently, with Koreans in the North—have contributed to more complex views of the diversity of "Koreans" both within and outside the Korean peninsula.

In the chaos of Korea's sudden liberation from Japanese colonial rule, returning political exiles helped to fill in the gap created by decades of colonial assimilation and oppression. There would have been sharp political differences among returnees under any circumstances, but the U.S.-Soviet divided occupation of the Korean peninsula intensified and polarized these differences within and between the two zones. Not surprisingly,

American-educated and English-speaking Koreans were favored in U.S.-controlled South Korea, while Koreans with Soviet (and Chinese) experience disproportionately benefited from the Soviet occupation in the North. The Soviets had the advantage of a larger number of cadres on "their" side— dozens of Russian-speaking ethnic Koreans, many of them second-generation Soviet citizens, were brought in to help build the North Korean regime between 1945 and 1948. The Americans had no equivalent cadre of Korean-Americans, but Korean returnees from the United States and Koreans educated by Americans within Korea played an important role in assisting the occupation and creating the South Korean regime. The leaders of the two Korean states established in 1948 testify dramatically to this: Syngman Rhee, who had spent most of his years since 1910 in the United States; and Kim Il Sung, who had lived almost exclusively in China (and briefly in Russia) since the age of twelve.

The two Korean states were each oriented toward their respective Great Power benefactors, and in close contact with the ethnic Korean communities therein—North Korea to China and the USSR, South Korea to the United States. Japan, although nominally a quasi-ally of South Korea after the Korean War, was a special case, as we shall see. During the height of the Cold War from the late 1940s to the 1980s, there was little contact among ethnic Korean communities across the Cold War divide. But as this divide began to weaken in the mid-1980s, the relationships among various ethnic Korean communities with each other and with the two Korean states became more complex and fluid.

Zainichi: Koreans in Japan

The effect of Korea's division on Koreans abroad has been most dramatic in Japan. In no other country with a large Korean minority has this community been so sharply divided as a result of the existence of two rival states on the peninsula. Two organizations, one pro-North and the other pro-South, have competed for the loyalty of Korean-Japanese since the late 1940s. Unlike other Western capitalist countries—and especially the United States—the Koreans in Japan have, until recently, been predominantly pro-North, for reasons of history, foreign policy, and the unique social circumstances of the Korean-Japanese. This split has even meant that what the Koreans, or Korea, are to be called is loaded with political significance: *Zainichi Chosenjin* or *Zainichi Kankokujin*. Both mean "Koreans residing in Japan," but the former uses the North Korean word for Korea (Chosŏn/Chosen), the latter the South Korean term (Hanguk/ Kankoku). Eventually, the Korean-Japanese managed to avoid the issue by simply calling themselves "Zainichi" (residents in Japan), everyone knowing who such residents are.

During the 1945–1952 U.S. occupation of Japan, the status of the Korean immigrants (and other non-Japanese residents) was ambiguous. Koreans, no longer citizens of a multi-ethnic empire, were not welcome in a supposedly "mono-ethnic" Japan.[24] The bulk of the Koreans chose to return to Korea. By 1948, only some 600,000 Koreans remained of the 2.4 million who had resided in Japan in August 1945. The majority of those who remained had immigrated before 1930, and had no place to return to—Japan was their home.[25] Under the terms of the San Francisco Peace Treaty that ended the American occupation in 1952, Koreans, Taiwanese, and Chinese in Japan became "third-country nationals"—neither Japanese nor foreigners—which did little to clarify their status. Civil war and political division in China and Korea made the "return" of such nationals problematic. Within Japan, left-wing activists played a prominent role in organizing the resident Koreans. The Zainichi Chosenjin Renmei (League of Korean Residents in Japan, or Choren), the leading Korean-Japanese association established after World War II, had close ties to the Japanese Communist Party and was favorably inclined toward North Korea. Pro-South Korean residents split with Choren and formed a rival organization, Zainichi Daikanminkoku Kyoryumindan (Community of Republic of Korea Residents in Japan, or Mindan). In 1955, Choren was supplanted by a new left-leaning organization, funded and supported by the North Korean government, called Zainichi Chosenjin Sorengokai (General Federation of Korean Residents in Japan, or Chosoren). Chosoren and Mindan remain fierce rivals for support among the Zainichi to this day. For the most of the period since 1955, however, Chosoren has been in the ascendancy.

The seeming paradox of a predominantly pro-North Korean ethnic community in an ostensibly pro-South Korean and U.S.-aligned Japan results from the discrimination Koreans face in Japan, and the success of North Korea (and conversely, the failure of South Korea) to exploit this discrimination in its favor. Under Syngman Rhee, President of South Korea from 1948 to 1960, the ROK did little to cultivate the support of ethnic Koreans in Japan. The DPRK, on the other hand, sent large-scale aid and accompanying propaganda to resident Koreans. In particular, the DPRK helped to build Korean-language schools in Japan, from the elementary level to a university, Korea University (Chosen Daikoku), an outpost of North Korean higher education on the outskirts of Tokyo.[26] The bulk of Korean-Japanese saw North Korea as a legitimate nationalist state, South Korea as a client of the United States. Even though most Zainichi had come originally from the southern part of the peninsula, when offered a choice between North and South Korean citizenship by the Japanese government in 1955, over 75 percent chose North Korean.[27] In the late 1950s the DPRK began negotiating with the Japanese government, through their respective Red Cross agencies (as the two countries lacked, and still lack, diplomatic relations) for the "repatriation" of Koreans to North Korea. For North Korea, this would help alleviate the DPRK's labor shortage as well as score a propaganda victory against the South. For Japan, it was a way to rid the country of a troublesome minority. In 1959, the first shipload of ethnic Koreans left Japan to settle in North Korea, where they were warmly welcomed by Kim Il Sung himself.[28]

By the time the program ended in 1984, over 100,000 ethnic Koreans from Japan—more than 80 percent of South Korea ancestry—had been "repatriated" to North Korea. For many, the DPRK's initial hospitality did not last long, and the favoritism showed the "returnees" in terms of jobs, housing, and social amenities created a backlash that sent more than a few to North Korean prison camps.[29] The precise fate of many of the repatriates, after their first few months or years in the DPRK, was often unknown to their relatives and friends in Japan. In particular, the conditions and treatment of the 6,755 Japanese spouses (mostly wives) of Koreans who went to the DPRK became a human rights issue in Japan in the 1970s and after.[30] None of these spouses was allowed to return to Japan until November 1997, when the DPRK government finally allowed a small group of Japanese wives to return to Japan for a two-week visit. While in Japan, the wives did not speak in detail publicly about their life in North Korea, and all returned.[31]

The Chosoren community in Japan has been a rare link between North Korea and the capitalist world, and thus an invaluable asset for the North Korean economy. For example, the business of running Japanese pachinko machines, a kind of vertical pinball game, is a virtual monopoly of Zainichi Koreans, and a substantial portion of pachinko profits—over a billion dollars a year, by one estimate—is funneled to North Korea.[32] Only in the 1990s, after the disintegration of the Soviet bloc, the economic collapse of the DPRK, and the rise of South Korea, did the political affiliations of the Zainichi shift away from North Korea toward the South. But by that time, a growing number of Korean Japanese, many now third- or fourth-generation residents in Japan, had opted to avoid the North-South choice altogether and obtain Japanese nationality.[33] The ability of either Korean state to maintain the loyalty of compatriots in Japan has since continued to decline.

Chosŏnjok: Koreans in China

The Koreans in Northeast China constitute the oldest, most self-contained, and until recently the largest community of ethnic Koreans outside the peninsula. As we have seen, after liberation in 1945, about half of the Koreans in Manchuria— close to a million people—chose not to return to Korea, having by this time settled permanently in Chinese territory. When the civil war between the Chinese Communists and Chiang Kai-shek's Nationalists erupted again in 1946, the majority of Koreans in China sided with the Communists. Ethnic Koreans had already dominated the Chinese Communist Movement in southern Manchuria before 1945, and many continued to fight alongside their ethnic Chinese counterparts during the Civil War period.[34] Unlike the nationalist Guomindang, the Chinese Communist Party (CCP) emphasized ethnic equality and autonomy for minority groups, and promised Koreans an active hand in local administration after a communist victory.

Both Northeast China and northern Korea were liberated by the Soviet army, and between August 1945 and the Korean War, the Sino-Korean border was relatively open. The status of the ethnic Koreans in Northeast China was ambiguous, and the Yanbian region was effectively an extension of Korea. This ambiguity remained after the establishment of the Democratic People's Republic of Korea (North Korea) in September 1948 and People's Republic of China (PRC) in October 1949; with the outbreak of the Korean War in 1950, however, the PRC made clear that the Koreans on the Chinese side of the Yalu and Tumen rivers owed their primary allegiance to China. The Koreans' status was confirmed by the creation of the Yanbian Korean Nationality Autonomous Region (*Yanbian Chaoxianzu Zizhiqu*) in September 1952, in the midst of the Korean War. In December 1955, Yanbian was administratively downgraded to an "Autonomous Prefecture" (*zizhizhou*) within the jurisdiction of Jilin Province. From this point onward, Koreans in the PRC would legally be considered "Chinese citizens of Korean nationality." While encouraged to maintain their ethnic identity, Koreans in China were expected to reserve their nationalist feelings for the Chinese state. "Our country" (*uri nara*), a term which for most Koreans abroad refers to Korea, meant for the Korean-Chinese the People's Republic of China.

Until about the mid-1980s, China's *Chaoxianzu* ("Korean nationality," *Chosŏnjok* in Korean pronunciation) was politically and culturally close to North Korea, and had little contact with—indeed, was officially quite hostile toward—South Korea. The term *Chosŏn* itself was the North Korean word for Korea, as opposed to *Hanguk*, the term used in South Korea. The Korean language used in China followed North Korean spelling and terminology, and the dialect spoken by the largest number of Koreans in China was that of the Hamgyŏng region in northern Korea, their ancestral homeland. Many ethnic Koreans had relatives across the border in North Korea, and were able to visit them fairly easily (although movement the other direction was more restricted). Like China as a whole, the ethnic Koreans publicly praised North Korean leader Kim Il Sung as a great patriot and independence fighter, albeit not with the degree of veneration the North Koreans themselves gave him. At the official level, China and North Korea were close allies throughout the Cold War period, sharing a "friendship cemented in blood" (to use a common Chinese slogan for the relationship) due to the Korean assistance to the communists in the Chinese Civil War and the Chinese participation in the Korean War. Under the surface, however, there were tensions in this relationship, and on occasion the ethnic Koreans became the victims of Sino-North Korean friction and political swings within China itself.

The PRC established an ethnic policy based largely on the Soviet model of officially recognized "nationalities," including the majority Han Chinese. Several of the largest minorities—the Mongols, the Tibetans, the predominantly Muslim Uighers, and the Zhuang of southwestern China—were granted "Autonomous Regions" at the administrative level of a province, although genuine local autonomy existed mostly on paper. Some smaller regions with predominantly non-Han populations were organized into autonomous prefectures, counties, and villages. In addition to the Yanbian Autonomous Prefecture, Korean autonomous areas included Changbaishan Autonomous County in the mountains of the Sino-Korean border, and several autonomous districts in Heilongjiang Province, Liaoning Province, and Inner Mongolia. At the beginning, Koreans in Yanbian were encouraged to maintain their language and culture, and held leading administrative positions in prefectural and city government. Like the country of Belgium or the Canadian province of New Brunswick, Yanbian is officially bilingual, with government documents and street signs in both Korean and Chinese. The administrative capital of Yanbian is the city of Yanji, a dusty provincial town far off the beaten path in Northeastern China, at least until it was discovered by South Korean tourists, investors, and missionaries in the 1980s and 1990s.

Minority groups were particularly vulnerable to the sudden "leftist" shifts in Chinese politics, which often contained a xenophobic element directed against non-Han ethnicities. Like other minorities, Koreans fell under suspicion as "local ethnic nationalists" during the Anti-Rightist Campaign of the late 1950s. Political persecution, combined with economic hardship following the Great Leap Forward famine of 1959–1960, motivated some ethnic Koreans to migrate across the border into North Korea, a movement at first welcomed by the Pyongyang government, as North Korea itself faced a perennial labor shortage. Many of these migrants returned to China after 1962, when political and economic conditions in China had stabilized.[35] Koreans faced even greater persecution and violent discrimination during the Cultural Revolution in the late 1960s, which was a disaster for China in general and devastating for China's minority groups in particular. The loyalty

Figure 4.1
Yanji, Capital of the Korean Nationality Autonomous Prefecture, Jilin Province, China.

of Koreans to the Chinese state was again called into question, as even China's relations with North Korea came under serious strain. Thousands of Koreans in Yanbian were killed or wounded in the violence of the Cultural Revolution, and tens of thousands were publicly humiliated, dismissed from their jobs, imprisoned, sent into internal exile, or otherwise persecuted. Institutes of higher learning in the Korean area especially suffered, as they did throughout China. Much of the faculty of Yanbian University, established in Yanji in 1949, was dismissed and sent to labor in the countryside. An ethnic Korean professor of Japanese language at Jilin University in Changchun, whom I met in the 1980s, recounted that during the Cultural Revolution he had been accused first of spying for Japan, then for South Korea, and finally for North Korea, and spent ten years cleaning toilets for his "crimes."

After the Cultural Revolution subsided in the late 1970s and China embarked on the path of economic reform under Deng Xiaoping, the situation of the Korean minority improved once again. For the most part, the Chosŏnjok have been an unproblematic group, even a "model minority." This is particularly visible in the area of education, where ethnic Koreans surpass the Han majority, and far surpass most minority groups, in their rate of graduation from institutes of higher learning, especially universities. Koreans' "education fever," so evident to observers of South Korea or the Koreans in the United States—where they are also over-represented in prestigious universities—is evident among Koreans in China as well.[36] Among the Han majority, Koreans in Northeast China had long held a reputation for valuing formal education, with every village household displaying the "Thousand-Character Classic" of traditional Chinese learning (Table 4.2).

The Chosŏnjok have found themselves in a new position as intermediaries between China and South Korea. After decades

Table 4.2 University Graduates in China per 10,000 Population, 1982

China	72.9
All minorities	31.6
Koreans	175.3

Source: Adapted from Chae-jin Lee, *China's Korean Minority:The Politics of Ethnic Education* (Boulder, CO: Westview Press, 1986), p. 7.

of official alignment with North Korea and isolation from the South, the Chosŏnjok developed a strong interest in South Korea during the 1980s, as China and the ROK opened up economic and cultural relations. Beginning in 1984, the ROK government welcomed "compatriots" from China to visit their relatives in South Korea. A trickle of visitors became a flood after the two countries established diplomatic relations in 1992. Many overstayed their visitor's visas and remained as illegal workers. The Chosŏnjok, most of them fluent in Korean and thus facing no language barrier, constitute the largest group of migrant workers in South Korea.

Koryŏ Saram: Koreans in the (former) USSR

After their deportation from the Russian Far East, the bulk of the Koreans in the USSR remained in Central Asia, where some 70 percent of the ethnic Koreans in the former Soviet Union still reside. Soviet Koreans played a key role in the creation of the DPRK, although many were purged from the political leadership after the Korean War. Using nationalism as a weapon, Kim Il Sung attacked his real and potential rivals for their alleged pro-Soviet or pro-Chinese sympathies, based on their backgrounds in the USSR or the Chinese Communist Movement, in the 1950s and 1960s.[37] Many of these purged cadres returned to the Soviet Union and China, where they became reintegrated into the local Korean communities. But the vast majority of ethnic Koreans in the USSR had no such political ties, and their connections to North Korea (or for that matter South Korea) were usually weak or nonexistent. Unlike Northeast China or Japan, Central Asia is a long way from Korea. And unlike in Chinese and Japanese, the word for "Korea" in Russian, the language of their host country (although not, of course, in Korean) had no political connotation. Nevertheless, Koreans in the USSR and post-Soviet republics have chosen generally to refer to themselves as "*Koryŏ saram*"—people of Koryŏ, the Korean kingdom that predated Chosŏn, and an ancient term for Koreans in general—rather than "*Chosŏn saram*" (North Korean) or "*Hanguk saram*" (South Korean). After the breakup of the Soviet Union, the Soviet Korean newspaper *Lenin kich'i* (Flag of Lenin) was renamed *Koryŏ Ilbo* (Korea Daily).[38]

Contrary to the expectations of South Korean business and government elites who had hoped the ethnic Koreans could serve as mediators for Korean investment in Russia, most *Koryŏ saram* chose to remain in Central Asia after the collapse of the USSR. A large-scale return to the Russian Far East never happened. After all, immigration from Korea into Russia had effectively ceased in 1937, and by the 1990s Koreans in the former USSR were third-, fourth-, or even fifth-generation Soviets. Probably more than any other major overseas Korean group, the Koreans in the USSR had assimilated into the host culture; most did not speak Korean. This meant that after the Central Asian republics gained their independence, ethnic Koreans occupied a somewhat ambivalent position, neither Russian nor members of the predominant local ethnic group—Kazakh, Uzbek, or whatever the case may be. It appears that, on the whole, the Koreans have adjusted to their position in the newly independent republics without great difficulty. Certainly, it helps not to be part of the once-dominant Russian minority.

A more recent group of Korean immigrants to the Soviet Union are the Koreans of Sakhalin Island. Brought in to work in the coal mines of southern Sakhalin when it was part of the Japanese empire, the Sakhalin Koreans mostly came from the southern part of the Korean peninsula. When World War II ended, the Sakhalin Koreans were left in a legal limbo. Not being Japanese, they were not repatriated on Allied vehicles to their homeland. Not being Russian, they were treated as foreigners by the Russians who took back the island. Thousands of Koreans remained in Sakhalin, stateless and ignored by both Korean governments for decades. In 1992, after South Korea and Russia had established diplomatic relations and the Sakhalin-Koreans could hold some hope of returning to Korea, the ROK government belatedly began to bring some of these "overseas compatriots" back to South Korea.[39]

Korean Americans: Koreans in the United States since 1953

After the anti-Asian Immigration Act of 1924, Koreans were not allowed to immigrate to the United States until 1952, during the Korean War. For the next thirteen years, most of the Koreans who came to the United States were either students, "G.I. brides" (Korean women married to American servicemen) and their families, or children adopted by Caucasian American parents. The immigration laws introduced by President Johnson in 1965, which opened the doors to immigrants from Asia and Latin America wider than ever before, radically changed the scope and character of the Korean American community. After 1965, large numbers of Korean families began to immigrate to the United States for economic opportunities, and especially for the education of their children. Korean immigration to the United States reached a peak between 1985 and 1987, with some 35,000 arrivals per year, making Korea the third-largest source of immigrants in the United States, after Mexico and the Philippines.[40]

Unlike many other immigrant groups (Cubans being perhaps the closest parallel), Koreans coming to the United States tended to be highly educated, urban, middle-class, and politically conservative. Korean immigrants were also disproportionately Christian. While 25 to 30 percent of South Koreans claimed to be Christian, the proportion was on the order of 80 percent among Korean Americans, the vast majority of these being Protestant. Partly this was because Korean Christians within Korea had ties with the United States through their churches and missionary contacts, and were therefore more likely to emigrate to America. Partly, this over-representation of Christians resulted from the church becoming the main center of social life in the Korean American community. Even if one didn't attend church in Korea, there were strong motivations to attend after coming to America—for making business contacts, finding a spouse, and cultivating an active community life, if not for religious reasons alone.

By the early 2000s, at least according to some accounts, Korean Americans had surpassed Korean Chinese as the largest community of "Overseas Compatriots," numbering over two million. Southern California, and especially Los Angeles, attracted the greatest concentration of Korean Americans, although large numbers also settled in New York, Chicago, and other major cities. Yet mainstream America seemed little aware of the Korean American community until the Los Angeles riots of 1992, when images of Korean shop-owners clashing with black and Latino looters in the chaos of South Central LA stunned television viewers throughout the nation. Many Korean Americans saw the LA riots as a turning point in the history of the Korean immigrant community. A relatively insular, almost invisible minority had been thrust into the middle

Figure 4.2
Koreatown, New York, USA.

of America's "first multi-ethnic riots;" as the Asian-American literature scholar Elaine Kim described it; for Korean Americans the LA riots were "a baptism into what it really means for a Korean to become American in the 1990s." [41] Some 2,280 Korean American-owned shops were looted and Korean American businesses suffered $400 million in damage.[42] One young Korean American man was killed. But beyond the physical and financial toll, the psychological effects of the riots were far-reaching. Korean Americans were forced to situate themselves on the fault lines of America's racial divide, and for many their faith in the American dream of unlimited opportunity had been severely tested, if not destroyed. For a time at least, the aftermath of the LA riots gave new energy to the Korean American community for promoting intra-ethnic solidarity within their own group, and multi-ethnic coalition-building with others. The second-generation Korean Americans took the lead in this, signaling the emergence of Koreans from a quiet, self-contained immigrant group to an active part of the American multi-ethnic dynamic.

Edward Taehwan Chang points out that the Korean American community is highly "bimodal"—divided sharply along lines of birthplace, language, culture, custom, and identity.[43] All these differences stem ultimately from the most glaring divide in this community, that of generations. First-generation Korean immigrants often do not even share a language with their children born in America: the former speak Korean, the latter English. Between are the so-called "1.5 Generation," those born in Korea who came to the United States as children or young adults, who sometimes form a bridge between the first and second generations, or just as often find themselves poised awkwardly between the two. Among other things, generational divide has made political cohesion among Korean Americans as a group difficult: members of the older generation are overwhelmingly conservative, viscerally anti-North Korean, and support the Republican Party; younger Korean Americans are more liberal, somewhat less hostile to North Korea (though very few are openly sympathetic), and are as likely to vote Democratic as they are to vote Republican. Partly because of these political differences, as well as a reluctance to become involved in American politics in general, Korean Americans thus far have had little success in forming an ethnic lobbying group in Washington, as have, for example, Irish and Cuban Americans.

That said, the Korean American community—the youngest of the four major overseas Korean communities—is changing rapidly. The stereotype of the first-generation male Korean immigrant who came in the 1960s or 1970s, a stereotype based largely on fact, is that of a white-collar professional with a high school or university education in South Korea, who faced severe downward mobility after coming to America. Establishing a small business such as a laundry, green-grocer, or liquor store, the immigrant, and his family would work impossibly long hours in order one day to send the children to the best universities in the United States. The children understood implicitly their obligation, and a disproportionate number did go to the top universities, usually to study practical, prestigious, and lucrative subjects such as medicine or engineering. With the passing of time, younger Korean Americans are going into other professions, such as teaching, law, and the arts. Unlike their parents, who came to America at a time of blatant racial discrimination and largely negative images of Asians in general, and (to the extent such images existed) of Koreans in particular, those born in the 1970s and 1980s have come of age at a time when Korean culture from South Korea is taking mainstream America by storm, and the talent and drive of Korean Americans is becoming increasingly apparent in many areas of American life, not least the universities. The impact of Korean Americans is just beginning to be felt in such fields as law, television and film acting, and business, to name only a few. Doubtless, much more is yet to come.

ADOPTED KOREANS

Koreans adopted by foreigners and living abroad, initially in the United States in the 1950s but later dispersed among many European countries and Canada as well, constitute a special group of "overseas Koreans," not easily categorized as migrants in an ordinary sense. Foreign adoption began shortly after the Korean War, initiated by the Oregon farmer and entrepreneur Henry Holt. Holt, who adopted eight Korean children of his own, was particularly concerned about the children of U.S. soldiers and Korean mothers left behind in Korea, children who would face a future of profound discrimination, fatherless and ethnically "other" in a society that put a high value on patrilines and ethnic homogeneity.[44] Partly as a result of Holt's lobbying, and with the support of notable public figures such as the novelist Pearl S. Buck, Congress authorized an "Operation Baby-Lift" that brought hundreds of mixed-race children of the Korean War to American military families in Japan between 1956 and 1959.[45]

At first, Holt's program focused on "Amerasian" children abandoned by their G.I. fathers, estimated to number over 1,000 at the end of the war (the total number of war orphans was probably well in excess of 250,000). Over time, the Holt Agency expanded to full-blooded Korean children given up for adoption by their parents. The Holt Agency and the Pearl S. Buck Foundation became the largest organizations for overseas adoption in Korea. As late as the 1980s, South Korea was among the largest sources of adoption for Americans; for the South Korean government, this high rate of adoption seemed a holdover for wartime poverty, and was something of an embarrassment to a country celebrating its affluence. After coming to office in 1998, President Kim Dae Jung publicly apologized to a group of overseas adoptees for his country's inability to take care of them. In recent years the South Korean government, as well as the adoption agencies themselves, have sponsored cultural education visits and family reunions for Koreans adopted abroad.

Large numbers of impoverished and abandoned children being adopted by foreigners in the aftermath of a devastating war is one thing, but the continuation of such high numbers of adoption by overseas families well into the period of South Korea's advanced economic development is an anomaly. South Korea's rates of foreign adoption, at least until recently, were comparable to places like China, Russia, and Romania, countries with much greater poverty and social dislocation. Much of this may be explained culturally, as the stigma against children born out of wedlock is still quite strong in Korea, and the traditional emphasis on blood ties has made Koreans generally reluctant to adopt children outside the extended family. This, along with the belief that sending children to be adopted by foreigners (meaning, especially, Americans) would give children a better life in the West, has motivated many impoverished and/or unmarried Korean mothers to give up their children to foreign adoption agencies. But of course, this option would not have been possible without the existence of such institutions in South Korea, where they have operated now for half a century. Cultural biases against domestic adoption, combined with the institutionalization of foreign adoption, have created an adoption "export industry" in South Korea unique among advanced industrial economies (Table 4.3).

North Korea also had large numbers of war orphans, but approached the problem quite differently. In keeping with the much more paternalistic state of the DPRK, North Korea insisted on taking care of its own orphans, largely through a system of state-run orphanages. The main orphanage in Pyongyang, the Mangyŏngdae Orphanage for Children of Revolutionary Martyrs, was founded by Kim Il Sung in 1948 for the offspring of his Manchurian guerilla compatriots who

Table 4.3   Korean Adoptees By Host Country

Country	Date Range	Adopted Koreans
United States	1953–1957	1,224
United States	1958–2001	97,837
France	1968–2001	10,923
Sweden	1957–2001	8,622
Denmark	1965–2001	8,417
Norway	1956–2001	5,806
Netherlands	1969–2001	4,056
Belgium	1969–1995	3,697
Australia	1969–2001	2,837
Germany	1965–1996	2,351
Canada	1967–2001	1,543
Switzerland	1968–1997	1,111
Luxembourg	1984–2001	418
Italy	1965–1981	382
England	1958–1981	72
Other countries	1956–1957	4
Other countries	1960–1995	62
Total	1953–2001	149,362

Source: http://en.wikipedia.org/wiki/International_
adoption_of_South_Korean_children.

had been killed in the struggle against Japanese colonialism. After the Korean War, the Mangyŏngdae Orphanage took in children of those killed in that war as well. During the war itself, thousands of children were taken in by East European families, including 1,500 in Romania alone.[46] Most of these children were brought back to North Korea after the completion of the 1957–1961 Five-Year Economic Plan, at which time North Korea declared its post-war reconstruction complete.

One can only imagine the heartrending scenes of European families forced to give up the Korean children they had raised, in many cases, for over a decade.

KOREANS AND THE MOTHERLAND

Modern Korean emigration has lasted almost a century and a half. The oldest Korean communities outside the peninsula, in China and Russia, are now into the fifth generation. The youngest large community of overseas Koreans, that of the United States, has also become the largest, and while two-thirds of today's Korean Americans were born in Korea, a growing proportion were born or lived all of their conscious lives in the United States. For all such communities, attachment to the country of residence and country of ancestry coexist, complementing or contradicting each other in a balance that varies across time and between individuals. Whether they migrated for reasons of economic desperation, educational opportunity, political necessity, or by colonial fiat, overseas Koreans have faced, at different times and in different forms, discrimination, suspicion, pressure for assimilation, and barriers to integration. Forced deportation in the Soviet Union, persecution during the Chinese Cultural Revolution, racism in the United States, and ethnic marginalization in Japan have been among the traumas faced by the Korean diaspora. Yet in many cases— indeed, at times precisely *because* of such discrimination—overseas Koreans have managed to retain the language, food, and customs of their ancestors across generations, continents, and oceans. All the while, the ancestral country itself underwent profound modern transformations that have changed it almost beyond recognition. A native of Seoul who emigrated to the United States in the 1960s, for example, and did not return until the 1980s—not an uncommon occurrence—would find the city bewildering, with hardly anything remaining of the Seoul he had left behind two decades earlier. The shock of the unfamiliar would be even greater for overseas Koreans returning from China or the former Soviet Union. But Korea is also a divided country, and North Korean refugees in the South face cultural adjustments at least as great as Koreans from abroad, if not greater. Seoul's ambition to be the capital of the "Korean National Community," to use former South Korean president Roh Tae Woo's phrase for the people of the peninsula and their overseas compatriots, must be tempered by the recognition that the motherland is a strange and unfamiliar place for many it would claim as its own.[47]

Throughout the diaspora, including the United States, writers, artists, and scholars of the various Korean communities have looked back to the motherland and tried to situate themselves in relation to it. One recent example is the work of Korean American poet Suji Kwock Kim. In her *Notes From the Divided Country*, the first book by a Korean American author to win the Walt Whitman Award of the Academy of American Poets, Kim reflects on the deep yet ambiguous connection between an "overseas Korean" and her ancestral land. Speaking for all children of the Korean diaspora, Kim says in "Translations from my Mother Tongue"—a poem about both mother and motherland:

Not much lives on, from one generation
to the next. Not much, but not
nothing: maybe the Paektu mountain tune
You both loved, crags grizzled with pine, rock maple,
black walnut, their burred and scabrous spines.

Shagbark or needledust. Gingkos scoured by snow.
Or cabbage chopped and scummed with pepper,
stocked in clay vessels, rocked into the soil like seeds.
Buried in fall, dug up in spring, soured, spiced,
to nourish and to burn. Tell me if this is true.[48]

A Korean folk tune, images of the Korean landscape, the recipe for *kimchee*—such fragile fragments of ancestral memory have been scattered across the modern world through the Korean diaspora.

Five

The Korean Crisis

The two Koreas were born in crisis. The promise of liberation from Japanese colonial rule in 1945 was quickly overshadowed by the political division of the country into two mutually antagonistic states in 1948. Just two years later, the Korean War—a devastating but localized hot war in the emerging global Cold War—solidified that division, and consolidated the two Korean regimes in their respective Cold War blocs. Ever since, and despite the termination of the Cold War as a global conflict in the early 1990s, the Korean peninsula has been a tinderbox of military confrontation, one of the few places in the world where a local conflict could draw in major nuclear-armed states and lead to a region-wide war. Nowhere else on earth has national division been so acute, antagonism so bitter, cross-boundary contact so limited, or mutual suspicion so high as on the Korean peninsula. Despite substantial progress toward peaceful coexistence (to use a classic Cold War phrase) since the early 1970s, when Sino-U.S. rapprochement opened up the space for North-South contacts on the Korean peninsula, the two Koreas remain on a semi-war footing. The existence of such national division and armed confrontation in a post-Cold War world seems paradoxical, but the still-unresolved Korean crisis arose from the specific encounter between local Korean conditions and the contradictory and uneven forces of globalization, a mix that has had particularly disastrous results for Korean peace and unity. For over fifty years, the Korean crisis has merely been contained; resolution, despite several promising beginnings, has yet to be achieved. In other words, the crisis of Korean division is not merely an epiphenomenon of the Cold War. Rather, it has its own peculiar dynamic, at the intersection of the global and the local.

In this chapter we will move from the perspective of each Korean state separately to examine the interaction of the two Korean regimes with each other, and the peninsula as a whole with the changing regional and global order since the Korean War. Each of the two Korean states has responded to the challenges of globalization not merely as an independent entity, but also—perhaps especially—in the context of a divided peninsula, each regime warily watching the other, existing in a state of hostile interdependence.[1] Neither Korea would have evolved as it has without the threat from, and competition with, the other; nor would the Korean crisis have remained so intractable were it not for the regional and global conditions that have so far blocked either a peaceful or violent end to Korean division.

FROM CONFRONTATION TO CAUTIOUS COEXISTENCE

From the time the two Korean states were founded in 1948, they have vied with each other for domestic legitimacy and international recognition. The Korean War could have resolved these claims for one side or the other, but the 1953 armistice left the two regimes in place, and they remained even more hostile toward each other than before. But after the early 1970s, when changes in regional and global politics opened the first space for tentative contact between the two regimes, inter-Korean relations have moved fitfully and gradually toward cautious coexistence. This process accelerated from the end of the 1990s, and may point toward an eventual peaceful resolution of the current state of confrontation on the Korean peninsula. Whether, or when, this leads ultimately to unification—the stated goal of both regimes, and the hope of many Koreans North and South—remains to be seen.

Seoul-Pyongyang relations have developed in four stages: the first stage, characterized by a zero-sum game of mutual antagonism, ended with the July 4 Communique of 1972, on the basis of which Seoul and Pyongyang for the first time established official contacts. The second stage, a period of on-again, off-again talks and exchanges, culminated in the 1991 Basic Agreement on Reconciliation, Non-Aggression, Exchanges and Cooperation, the 1992 agreement on de-nuclearization of the Korean Peninsula, and the entry of the two Korean states simultaneously into the United Nations in September 1992. Both the 1972 and 1991–1992 agreements raised high hopes for reconciliation and reunification on the Korean peninsula, but such hopes were soon overtaken by renewed distrust and mutual hostility. In the late 1990s, after a period of severe domestic crisis in North Korea coinciding with a nuclear stand-off with the United States, a third stage began with the tentative opening of North Korea to external economic and political forces, culminating in the June 2000 Pyongyang summit meeting between North Korean leader Kim Jong Il and South Korean President Kim Dae Jung. But the expectations raised by this historic summit and the evolving rapprochement between the United States and North Korea faced a setback with the coming of the more hawkish Bush administration, and a second nuclear crisis between the United States and North Korea erupted in the fall of 2002.

Finally, inter-Korean relations have most recently entered a fourth stage, a period of intensifying economic linkages within the broader framework of an evolving regional dialogue among the two Koreas, Russia, China, Japan, and the United States. This dialogue, the so-called Six-Party Talks, begun in 2003 in response to the U.S.-North Korean nuclear confrontation, achieved a formal agreement in September 2005, but had little concrete effect on resolving the Korea problem. Nevertheless, the multilateral discussion held the potential to create a more stable regional environment in Northeast Asia, allowing inter-Korean integration to continue and deepen. Despite the inability to resolve the nuclear standoff between North Korea and the United States, whether through bilateral or multilateral means, inter-Korean relations by the mid-2000s were more extensive and advanced than at any time in the history of divided Korea. Barring a renewed war on the peninsula, the sudden collapse of the North Korean regime, or other unexpected event, the trend toward greater interaction, interdependence, and integration between the two Koreas will continue. Unification as such, however, may yet be many years away.[2]

THE TWO KOREAS IN THE COLD WAR

From the late 1940s until the early 1970s—that is, from the beginning of the Cold War to Sino-American rapprochement—inter-Korean relations were characterized by an existential antagonism in which each Korean state saw its rival as a threat to its own existence, and held as its explicit goal the elimination of the other. Only once, in the summer and fall of 1950, did the Koreas put this existential antagonism into military practice. Both nearly succeeded, one after the other: the Korean People's Army of North Korea conquered and controlled most of the South between June and September 1950; after the UN intervention in mid-September, South Korean, U.S., and UN forces wrested most of the territory of North Korea from DPRK control between October and December that year. But by early 1951, after the Chinese intervention and UN counterattack, the Korean War had become a stalemate. The armistice signed in July 1953 established this stalemate as a permanent condition. From that point onward neither Korean side attempted to invade the other, both restrained by their respective Great Power patrons.[3]

For two decades, the two Koreas reflected almost perfectly the symmetrical standoff between the superpowers. The Korean peninsula was the Cold War in microcosm, each regime threatening the other with mutually assured destruction at the local level, just as the Soviet Union and United States did at the global level. However, this apparent symmetry belied very different dynamics within the two sides of the conflict. In particular, the Sino-Soviet split on the communist side gave North Korea room to maneuver and the opportunity to play off its two patrons against each other to its own advantage. South Korea, part of a much more unilateral U.S. hegemony, had no such space for independent action, and given its bitter history with Japan was not about to court Japan at the expense of America, as North Korea would play off China against the USSR. Perhaps ironically, in the long run this helped to make North Korea less flexible internally, as neither China nor the USSR was willing to push the DPRK too hard for domestic reform lest Pyongyang threaten to "defect" to the other patron. On the other hand, South Korea, as we have seen, did eventually evolve toward political democracy and develop a world-class industrial economy in part through American aid and pressure—although the bulk of credit for these accomplishments must go to the Koreans themselves.

North Korea and the Sino-Soviet Split

The heyday of "socialist brotherhood" among the USSR, China, and North Korea did not long outlive the Korean War. The competition between China and the USSR for leadership of global communism became increasingly apparent in the late 1950s, leading to an open rift between the two countries by 1960. The Sino-Soviet split could have been disaster for North Korea, but instead of taking sides in the conflict, North Korea managed to manipulate the competition between its two major power patrons to its own advantage. China's criticism of Khrushchev's de-Stalinization campaign, opposition to détente with the West, support for Third World revolution, and promotion of rapid industrialization internally gave the PRC a great deal in common with North Korea, and during this period Sino-North Korean relations were particularly close. But North Korea was also dependent on the USSR for economic and military aid, and was wary of alienating Moscow. Alone among smaller communist countries caught up in the Sino-Soviet split, the DPRK managed to maintain a rough balance between the two communist giants throughout the three decades of Sino-Soviet alienation. It is not so much that North Korea "leaned toward" one or the other of its patrons, although at times it did, but rather that the DPRK maintained a certain distance from both while gaining from each the benefits of its strategic position vis à vis the other. In this respect the DPRK was a shrewd practitioner of what Annette Baker Fox has called "the power of small states," playing off the competition between its two much larger neighbors for its own benefit.[4]

Soviet and Chinese policies in East Asia were becoming more divergent than complementary by the latter 1950s.[5] At the heart of this division was the contrast between Mao's "anti-imperialism" and Khrushchev's "peaceful co-existence" with the West. The rumblings of this clash could already be heard in 1957, although few in the West recognized this at the time. By the end of the decade, the split within the communist world would come out into the open, and the DPRK had to tread a careful path along the rift. But unlike North Vietnam, for example, with which North Korea shared some obvious parallels, the DPRK never fell fully into the "Soviet camp" nor clashed directly with China.

While publicly on good terms, in reality the Soviet and PRC governments, and Mao and Khrushchev personally, were at odds by the summer of 1958. The immediate cause of the conflict was a pair of Soviet proposals that Mao seemed to take as direct affronts to Chinese sovereignty: building a radio station in China to keep track of American naval activities in the Pacific; and creating a joint Sino-Soviet submarine flotilla under Soviet command. On July 22, Mao invited Soviet Ambassador Yudin to discuss the latter issue. The discussion quickly became a rant on the part of Mao about Soviet anti-Chinese prejudice and Great Power chauvinism. The Soviets had "extend[ed] Russian nationalism to China's coast," Mao claimed, and he told Yudin "You have never had faith in the Chinese people, and Stalin was among the worst."[6] Khrushchev flew to Beijing to calm the waters, meeting with Mao on July 31. But the damage had already been done, and Sino-Soviet relations were on a rapid downhill spiral from July 1958 onward.

In early September, Soviet Foreign Minister Gromyko visited Beijing in the midst of the PRC shelling of Quemoy and Matsu in the Taiwan Straits, making no secret of Soviet disapproval of China's "adventurism" (although the Soviets were applying similar brinkmanship tactics over Berlin).[7] In early October 1959, Khrushchev met with U.S. President Eisenhower, a major boost to "peaceful co-existence," while China still took an official anti-imperialist position and was beginning to feel the disastrous effects of the Great Leap Forward. In the Sino-Indian border conflict of September to October 1959, the Soviet Union took a neutral position and was sharply criticized for this in China. By the time Khrushchev and Mao met again in Beijing for the tenth anniversary of the founding of the PRC in October 1959, the stage was set for all-out confrontation between the two communist giants.[8]

The sudden withdrawal of Soviet specialists from China in July 1960 brought the Sino-Soviet conflict into the open for the world to see. North Korea refused publicly to takes sides at this point. While North Korean state media did not support the post-Stalin reforms in the USSR, it was also critical of the PRC, albeit not always directly. For example, the KWP Central Committee in October 1960 criticized obsequious attitudes toward foreign countries and mindless imitation of things foreign, a practice which it labeled *sadaejuŭi*, or "flunkeyism" as it was officially translated in later North Korean texts. This term cropped up in numerous party publications and speeches by officials over the next several months, and the "factionalists" of 1956 were also accused of practicing *sadaejuŭi*.[9] Both pro-Soviet and pro-Chinese behavior was condemned as "flunkeyism," but for Korean and Chinese readers, it was obvious that *sadaejuŭi* referred to Korea's traditional reverence for China and Chinese culture—the term "Sadae" or "Serving the Great" originated with the ancient Chinese philosopher Mencius, and in traditional Korea referred to Korea's subordinate relationship to China. *Sadaejuŭi* was, in fact, the antithesis of *juche*, dependence rather than self-reliance. The use of this term implied that *juche* would not only be directed against the Soviet Union, which was the primary target of Kim's original 1955 *juche* speech (see Chapter 3), but against any dependence on or imitation of China as well.

Albania, of all countries, played an important symbolic role in dramatizing North Korea's position vis à vis the Soviet Union and China. At the Moscow Conference of Communist Parties in December 1960, where the Soviet-Albanian clash became a kind of substitute for the Sino-Soviet conflict, the North Korean delegation refused to take sides in the dispute. On the other hand, publications within North Korea around the same time praised Albania as a successful independent socialist country. For example, the DPRK newspaper *Minju Chosŏn* said in November 1960 that "our two countries are very close to each other, like real brothers, because of common ideology and aims ... no force on earth can break the invincible friendship and solidarity between the Korean and Albanian people."[10] North Korean-Albanian ties became extremely close in 1960–1962, with frequent exchanges of delegations, and new agreements on technical assistance, trade, and cultural cooperation. On the one hand, the DPRK was not willing to risk an open confrontation with the USSR; on the other hand, its "real" sympathies seemed to lie more with Albania, another small socialist country on the periphery of the Soviet empire, and with China, with whom it shared a common view of revolution and anti-imperialism.

The Soviets, for their part, were not willing to "lose" North Korea to Chinese influence, nor risk the DPRK leaving the Soviet orbit as Albania and Yugoslavia had. Neither, however, was the USSR under Khrushchev willing to support North Korea to the point of provoking a confrontation with the United States. As we have seen, there was a degree of symmetry between the Soviet position and that of the United States, which was concerned throughout the Syngman Rhee period, and probably beyond, of a South Korean provocation that would draw the United States into another war on the Korean peninsula. The stalemate of the war had evolved into a status quo that, though potentially volatile, was sustainable and not likely to be broken by either of the main Cold War protagonists. Kim Il Sung had little choice but to accept this status quo, although he must have found it deeply frustrating. The Soviets would give the DPRK enough military and economic aid to keep it going, but not enough to encourage North Korea to conquer the South.

Khrushchev's "peaceful co-existence" was perceived by the DPRK leadership as little short of capitulation to the Americans, a policy that would undermine North Korea's position vis à vis the South. In September 1959, Khrushchev visited the United States for his famous visit with Eisenhower. The fact that Khrushchev went to the United States first, before visiting the PRC, did not go down well with the Chinese, who were openly "enraged" at Khrushchev when the Soviet delegation reached Beijing in early October.[11] The North Koreans were reluctant to even publish the details of Khrushchev's visit to the United States, until pressured to do so by the Soviet embassy in Pyongyang.[12] And, to top it off, Khrushchev did not visit North Korea at this time, as he had proposed doing earlier in the year. The North Koreans had been preparing for Khrushchev's visit since the summer, and expected it to coincide with his visit to China in October. It would be the first visit by a top Soviet leader to the DPRK, and virtually the entire city of Pyongyang was mobilized to clean up the city and organize the welcoming parade. But at the last minute, Khrushchev informed the North Koreans from Beijing that he would not make it to Korea after all—in part, the Soviets implied, so as not antagonize the United States.[13] Although not an incident of great moment in concrete terms, this demonstration of insensitivity to the Koreans' pride served to reinforce the image of the Soviet Union, and Khrushchev personally, as a fickle and untrustworthy ally.

The 1960–1962 period was the one in which North Korea seemed to lean closest to China.[14] In fact, Sino-North Korean relations were not as close in practice as the rhetoric of both countries' propaganda would suggest. From a North Korean perspective, China had little to offer economically after the disaster of the Great Leap Forward. On the contrary, famine in China pushed tens of thousands of ethnic Koreans across the border into North Korea in the early 1960s.[15] Even more of China's Korean minority would flee across the border later in the decade, as a result of political and ethnic persecution during the Chinese Cultural Revolution, when Sino-Korean relations reached their nadir. Despite official praise for China's achievements during the Great Leap Forward, KWP internal statements were quite critical of the Chinese Communist Party (CCP) economic policies.[16] Chinese promises of economic assistance to North Korea after 1959 went mostly unfulfilled; quite literally, China could not deliver the goods, despite strenuous attempts on the part of the PRC to compete with the USSR in offering North Korea equipment, technical assistance, and entire factories for light-industry production.[17] But even if the economic benefits of relations with China showed limited returns in the early 1960s, China was still useful as a military and political balance against the USSR; on July 6, 1961, the DPRK signed a Treaty of Friendship, Cooperation and Mutual Assistance with the USSR in Moscow, and then, four days later, signed an almost identical treaty with China.[18]

We can see the period of the early 1960s as a time when North Korea carefully steered a course between the Soviet Union and China, a pattern that the DPRK would follow for most of the Cold War, until the Sino-Soviet split ended in 1989 with Gorbachev's visit to Beijing (in the midst of the Tiananmen crisis), followed by the Soviet collapse in 1991. There were zigzags in this relationship, but for the most part China offered more political and ideological support, the USSR more economic and military benefits. But above all, the falling out between the two communist giants convinced the DPRK leadership that neither could be relied on in the long term. Even within the communist world, juche was the logical way forward. According to East European reports, Kim told the KWP Central Committee in the spring of 1962 that the Soviet Union may one day cast aside the DPRK as they had Albania, and that the North Korean people must be prepared for such an eventuality.[19] North Korea would have to be self-reliant.

South Korea and the United States

Unlike North Korea, South Korea did not have two patrons in competition with one another. Japan was no China: the Japanese knew their place in the American-led East Asian regional order. South Korea was a client of the United States, with tens of thousands of American troops stationed within its borders. The North Korean government made much of this continued U.S. military presence, and never failed to point out that the last foreign soldiers in North Korea, the Chinese People's Volunteers, had left the country in 1958. Far from Japan and the United States competing for influence in South Korea, as China and the USSR did in the North, the ROK strongly resisted U.S. pressure to improve relations with Japan for almost two decades after liberation. Since well before the Korean War, U.S. policy planners had sought to integrate Japan and South Korea economically, as a central component of a reinvigorated East Asian regional economy.[20] Syngman Rhee, who if nothing else was viscerally anti-Japanese (which did not, however, prevent him from staffing his government with many former Japanese collaborators), refused to go along with this American vision and to normalize relations with Japan. Park Chung Hee was finally able to push through a normalization treaty in 1965, in the face of enormous popular protests and the resistance of the political opposition. This, too, was something the North Koreans could use as propaganda against the South: a South Korean president with a collaborationist past doing America's bidding by reestablishing ties to Japan. It was not quite so simple, of course, and as we have seen, normalization with Japan brought substantial economic benefits to South Korea.

The Vietnam War was also an economic boon to the South, if something of a political liability on the world stage. But Vietnam was important for the North as well, if only symbolically. Blocked from any significant direct engagement on the Korean peninsula itself, the two Koreas played out a kind of proxy war in Vietnam. The South Korean intervention on the American side in 1965 was condemned in the strongest possible terms by Pyongyang. The DPRK for its part sent medicines, clothes, and other goods to aid the South Vietnamese guerilla movement. In July 1965 North Korea offered to send the South Vietnamese resistance forces as much material aid and military equipment as they needed, and in January 1966 the DPRK and the Democratic Republic of Vietnam (DRV) concluded an "Economic Agreement on Free Aid." Throughout the Vietnam War North Korea continued to send aid to the DRV, although the precise amount is not known. Also in 1966, Kim Il Sung offered to send combat troops as well, but he was turned down.[21] Other than military advisors and perhaps some air support, it does not appear that the DPRK ever contributed its own military forces to the Vietnam War, in striking contrast to South Korea's 325,000 combat soldiers during its 1965–1973 intervention.

Thus, in the mid-1960s, North Korea was diverting precious resources to its defense build-up and even sending economic and military assistance to Vietnam, at the time when assistance from the socialist countries had largely disappeared. Meanwhile South Korea's policy of export-oriented economic development was beginning to bear fruit, and the Vietnam intervention also gave a huge boost to the South Korean economy in the form of American aid, loans, and payments to individual soldiers. In short, North Korea's foreign and domestic policies were putting a severe strain on its economy at precisely the moment when the South Korean economy, after nearly two decades of stagnation, was beginning to take off. In retrospect, we can see this as a turning point in the relative economic fortunes of the two Koreas. By the mid-1970s at the latest, South Korea would overtake the North economically, and the gap would grow increasingly in the South's favor over the next three decades.

CRACKS IN THE COLD WAR IMPASSE, 1972–1992

In the first half of the Cold War, the three major divided nations (Korea, China, and Germany) held similar policies of nonrecognition: the two Koreas, like the two Chinas and the two Germanies, refused to recognize their rival state's existence or to maintain diplomatic ties with any foreign country that did recognize it. Both Koreas were entrenched in their respective Cold War blocs, which reinforced the North-South Korean confrontation and inhibited North-South contact. This external environment changed dramatically in the early 1970s, when the Nixon administration made secret, and then public, overtures toward normalization with the People's Republic of China, North Korea's closest supporter. To preempt abandonment by their respective patrons, the two Koreas took matters into their own hands and began direct negotiations with each other, first through their respective Red Cross committees and then through a series of meetings between North and South Korean intelligence officers. Just under a year after Henry Kissinger's secret visit to Beijing on July 9, 1971, Seoul and Pyongyang issued a Joint Communiqué on July 4, 1972, outlining their principles for peaceful unification.

The new movement in inter-Korean relations inaugurated by the July 4 Communiqué raised tremendous expectations in both the North and the South, but produced little in the way of concrete result. After a half-dozen meetings of the newly created South-North Coordinating Committee, the two sides reached an impasse and the North cut off talks in mid-1973.[22] North-South Red Cross dialogue was revived in the mid-1980s and there was a brief flurry of cultural exchanges and visits of separated families in 1985, but this too quickly fizzled out. The next breakthrough in official inter-Korean relations would not come until the beginning of the 1990s, by which time the international environment had changed drastically, to the benefit of the South and the great detriment of the North.

The growing economic strength of South Korea in the 1980s found diplomatic expression in the Nordpolitik of President Roh Tae Woo in the latter part of the decade. Focused on wooing North Korea's communist allies into economic and political relations with the ROK, and modeled on West Germany's Ostpolitik toward East Germany and the Soviet bloc, Nordpolitik was extremely successful at establishing ties between South Korea and the communist countries in Eastern Europe, including the Soviet Union itself, which recognized the ROK in 1990. For the North, Roh outlined a broad vision of inter-Korean cooperation, and ultimately unification, into what he called a "Korean National Community."[23] The main North Korean proposal for unification, to which Roh's proposal was in part a response, was a "Confederation" of the two existing political systems on the Korean peninsula, first proposed in 1960. While initially presented as a sudden union of the two systems, over time the North has shown flexibility in its Confederation proposal, willing to see confederation not as the end-goal of unification but a transitory institution and giving more rights to the two "regional governments." By 1991, in fact, North Korean officials including Kim Il Sung were suggesting that there was room for negotiation with the South on the form of confederation and that both sides within a confederated Korean system could have considerable autonomy even in its foreign relations, under the general rubric of military and diplomatic unity.[24] This proposed "Confederal Republic of Koryŏ" was thus not dissimilar to Roh's "Korean National Community." Both proposals, however, remained fairly abstract; on the ground, inter-Korean relations moved cautiously toward government-to-government contacts.

As the 1990s dawned, high-level North-South talks began again. In December 1991, the fifth in this series of high-level talks produced an agreement on reconciliation, nonaggression, and exchanges and cooperation.[25] The "Basic Agreement" was the most important declaration of North-South cooperation and coexistence since the 1972 Joint Communiqué, and was far more detailed than the 1972 agreement had been. It was followed in February 1992 by a joint "Declaration of the Denuclearization of the Korean Peninsula." Once again, hopes were high for a major change in North-South relations and for a new momentum toward reconciliation and eventual unification. But once again such hopes would be unfulfilled. Regional and global circumstances had shifted dramatically, and the very survival of the North Korean regime became Pyongyang's preoccupation. Movement toward inter-Korean reconciliation would be postponed as North Korea went through a series of profound crises. The collapse of every communist state in Eastern Europe between 1989 and 1991, including the USSR itself, came as a deep shock to North Korea and deprived Pyongyang of most of its important trade partners, political supporters, and allies. Even before the communist collapse, East European countries had begun to normalize relations with the ROK; by 1992, Russia and even North Korea's allegedly staunch ally China had established diplomatic relations with Seoul. It would take almost a decade for a reciprocal movement of Western countries normalizing ties with Pyongyang. Economically, South Korea had long since leapt almost unimaginably beyond the level of the DPRK. Far from the Basic Agreement ushering in a new age of equality between the two Koreas, the times seemed to call into question the continued ability of the DPRK to exist at all. Movement in inter-Korean relations seemed almost a moot point. German-style unification, with the South absorbing the North as West Germany had absorbed East Germany in 1990, was widely predicted, especially by Western analysts.[26]

THE POST-COLD WAR CRISES

The collapse of communism in Europe and the end of the Cold War did not lead to a peaceful resolution of the Korea problem.[27] On the contrary, in the early 1990s, Korea—or more specifically, North Korea—became the site of one of the first crises of the post-Cold War era. After the Cold War, the American security policy became extremely concerned with so-called "rogue states"—small, highly authoritarian regimes with a history of hostility to the United States and other Western countries and the potential for producing "weapons of mass destruction" (biological, chemical, and especially nuclear weapons). In particular, Iraq and North Korea became the two places where the world's remaining superpower came most consistently to the point of military conflict. This occurred in both places, almost simultaneously, on two occasions: the Gulf War of 1990–1991, followed by a near-war over North Korea's nuclear program in 1993–1994; and the Iraq War of 2003, which occurred in the midst of a second North Korean nuclear crisis that began in October 2002.

Of course, in many respects the origins, nature, and (potential) resolution of these regional-cum-global conflicts are vastly different. The post-Cold War struggles in the Middle East, and the Persian Gulf in particular, are related to strategic natural resources, disputed post-colonial national boundaries, and religion, none of which have much relevance in Korea and Northeast Asia. The Middle East has been explosive, the site of continuous low-intensity warfare and terrorism when not embroiled in outright war; conflict on the Korean peninsula, since the Korean War armistice of July 1953, has been much more contained, despite the high level of constant tension. Nevertheless, whether as "rogue states" or members of the "axis of evil" (along with Iran), Iraq and North Korea tended to be viewed by post-Cold War U.S. policy-makers as regimes beyond the pale of normal diplomacy, oppressive toward their own people, and threatening to the stability of the international system.[28] The two regimes were certainly linked in the minds of U.S. political leaders and in the American media, if not in the states of concern themselves. The U.S. invasion and occupation of Iraq did little to change this negative appraisal of the DPRK, although military options for "regime change" in North Korea were tempered by the difficulties besetting American forces in Iraq after the 2003 invasion.

The First Nuclear Crisis and the Politics of Engagement

The collapse of communism in Eastern Europe and the dis-integration of the Soviet Union in 1989–1991 was a disaster for North Korea, both politically and economically. The very existence of the DPRK as a state appeared to be in doubt—many Western obeservers, and perhaps North Korea's leaders themselves, saw East Germany or Romania as North Korea's near-future—but the DPRK refused to accept such a fate. On the contrary, the regime's first response was to loudly declare its unwavering commitment to socialism, the "wave of the future."[29] It was in this context that North Korea pursued its nuclear program in the early 1990s, with nuclear weapons as a potential by-product useful for a defense against a hostile world—and against an American nuclear attack in particular. As the political scientist Paul Bracken has put it, the North Korean nuclear program was a way to "buy time for the regime to adapt to new international circumstances."[30] If so, the scheme backfired: American concerns about North Korea's nuclear program, and North Korea's refusal to allow inspections to determine whether or not it was diverting spent nuclear fuel into weapons production, brought the United States and North Korea to the brink of war in June 1994. A second Korean War was averted at the eleventh hour by the visit of former U.S. President Carter to Pyongyang to hold discussions with Kim Il Sung. This paved the way for direct talks between the U.S. and the DPRK, and although Kim died of a heart attack in July, these talks led to a "Framework Agreement" in October 1994 that froze North Korea's plutonium program in exchange for promises of energy aid from the West, and of movement toward normalization.[31] In the event, neither side completely kept to its promises, and the agreement collapsed in 2005.

Nuclear weapons were not a new aspect of the Korea problem. North Korea had lived under the threat of an American nuclear attack since the Korean War, and had long sought a deterrent against such an attack. Its main deterrence was its mutual defense treaty with the USSR, but an independent nuclear capability had probably been considered since well before the 1990s. The Soviet Union had assisted North Korea in the development of nuclear energy since the late 1950s, although it discouraged North Korea from developing nuclear weapons.[32] The Soviet Union and North Korea signed their first agreement on atomic energy cooperation in September 1959, and established North Korea's first nuclear research center and reactor in Yŏngbyŏn, about 100 kilometers north of Pyongyang (the very nuclear plant that aroused U.S. and international suspicion in 1993–1994). As a result of this agreement with Moscow, hundreds of North Korean nuclear specialists were trained in the Soviet Union, including many at the leading Soviet laboratories in Dubna. In the 1970s and 1980s, North Korea expanded its program of nuclear energy development, helped not just by Soviet advice and assistance but also by substantial deposits of natural uranium. The fact that Japan and South Korea were similarly developing nuclear energy on a large scale was no doubt a factor in this expansion. South Korea was also trying to develop nuclear weapons, until it was stopped by the United States in the early 1970s, which gave North Korea even more incentive to develop its own deterrent.

Soviet nuclear assistance to North Korea ended abruptly. In December 1985, the Soviet Union had agreed to help the DPRK construct a nuclear power plant near Sinp'o on the east coast of North Korea, but in 1992, North Korea's failure to pay for construction led Russia to halt work on the Sinp'o project, leaving the DPRK $1.7 million dollars in debt to Russia's atomic ministry. In April 1993, in the midst of the crisis with the United States and just after North Korea announced its intention to withdraw from the nuclear Non-Proliferation Treaty (NPT), Russian president Boris Yeltsin put a halt to all remaining Russian-North Korean nuclear cooperation activities.[33] The site near Sinp'o was the very same place where a U.S.-led consortium would propose building two nuclear reactors as part of the 1994 Framework Agreement. When that agreement broke down, with little more than holes in the ground where the reactors were to be built, the North Koreans could claim that they had been cheated out of nuclear power plants twice, first by the Russians and then by the Americans. Of course, North Korea's own cheating played no small part in the breakdown of both agreements. In any case, in 2003 North Korea again threatened to withdraw from the NPT, and this time it carried out the threat.

The 1994 Framework Agreement offered a "road map" for improved ties between the United States and North Korea, with diplomatic normalization as the potential end-product (indeed, the agreement specifically stated that the United States and North Korea would move toward normalization). At the time, the South Korean government under Kim Young Sam was suspicious of this agreement, reached by the United States and the DPRK without South Korea's direct participation. While U.S.-North Korean relations moved into uncharted territory that promised a new relationship, under the initiative of President Kim Dae Jung South Korea focused its attention again on expanding North-South ties. Elected president of the ROK in December 1997, Kim considered improvement of North-South relations as one of his highest priorities in office. His policy of stepping up economic and cultural ties with North Korea in the hopes that positive inducements would encourage internal reform and inter-Korean dialogue, dubbed the "Sunshine Policy," put Seoul in the lead in engagement with North Korea. The Clinton administration in the United States, despite the 1994 Agreed Framework, moved slowly and sporadically toward normalization with Pyongyang, not least because of a highly critical congress that came under Republican control a few weeks after the agreement was signed. North Korea's test-firing of a missile over Japan led to a new crisis in U.S.-DPRK relations in 1998, which led in turn to a renewed attempt at engagement. American engagement with Pyongyang reached a peak in the fall of 2000, when North Korean Vice-Marshal Jo Myong-rok, the de facto number-two ruler in Pyongyang, met with President Clinton in Washington. Shortly thereafter, Secretary of State Madeleine Albright met Kim Jong Il in Pyongyang. The two sides renewed their commitment to work toward normal relations, and North Korea appeared to be on the verge of agreeing to curtail its missile development and exports, one of Washington's chief concerns. But such promises could not come to fruition before Clinton left office, and the Bush victory in the 2000 presidential election effectively halted U.S. momentum toward normalization with the DPRK.

Meanwhile, inter-Korean relations reached new heights (at least symbolically) with the Kim Jong Il-Kim Dae Jung meeting in Pyongyang in June 2000. At the same time, and with Seoul's encouragement, North Korea began to emerge from its diplomatic isolation. In the space of two years, Pyongyang established diplomatic relations with most countries in Western Europe and Southeast Asia, along with Canada, Australia, the Philippines, Brazil, and New Zealand; in July 2000, North Korea joined the Asean Regional Forum (ARF) for East Asian security dialogue[34] Domestically, North Korea began to make cautious but potentially far-reaching steps toward internal economic reform, including unprecedented wage and price reforms undertaken in the summer of 2002.[35] Improvement in inter-Korean relations was part and parcel of this trend toward North Korea becoming a more "normal" country.

While North-South Korean relations were on a generally upward trend, U.S.-North Korean relations took a decided turn for the worse after George W. Bush became president. Bush condemned North Korea as part of an "Axis of Evil," along with Iran and Iraq, in his State of the Union address in January 2002. North Korea responded with predictable outrage. A Foreign Ministry spokesman called the Bush speech "little short of declaring war against the DPRK" and accused the U.S. administration of "political immaturity and moral leprosy."[36] North-South relations, having already lost a great deal of momentum since the summer of 2000, were dampened considerably by the Bush administration's statements. It took a visit to Pyongyang by Kim Dae Jung's special envoy Lim Dong Won in early April to get inter-Korean dialogue restarted. On April 28, Pyongyang agreed to resume reunion meetings of separated family members and to move forward with high-level contacts and economic cooperation. On August 11–14 the first ministerial-level North-South meetings in nearly a year took place in Seoul. At the same time, the two sides marked the 57th anniversary of liberation from Japanese colonial rule on August 15th with an unprecedented joint celebration, including the visit of more than one hundred North Korean delegates to Seoul.[37]

Washington-Pyongyang relations also showed signs of thaw in late July and early August 2002, when Secretary of State Colin Powell met briefly with North Korea's foreign minister at an Asean meeting in Brunei, and the Bush Administration sent Jack L. Pritchard as its first official envoy to the DPRK. Pritchard, who had met with Pyongyang's ambassador to the UN several weeks earlier in New York, went to North Korea in early August for the ceremony marking the start of construction on the first light-water nuclear reactor to be built by the Korean Peninsula Energy Development Organization (KEDO), the U.S.-South Korean-Japanese consortium formed under the auspices of the 1994 Agreed Framework.[38] And on the DPRK-Japan side, Prime Minister Koizumi's unprecedented summit meeting with Kim Jong Il in Pyongyang in September, where Kim made his extraordinary admission that North Korea had abducted over a dozen Japanese citizens in the 1970s and 1980s, seemed at first to open up a new era in Japan-North Korea relations and start the two countries on the road to normalization.[39] Kim Jong Il's revelations, presumably intended to clear the path for DPRK-Japan normalization, had the opposite effect: the Japanese media and public responded to these revelations such feelings of hostility toward North Korea that the "abduction issue" became a major impediment to improved ties between North Korea and Japan.

The Second Nuclear Crisis

The belated and tentative moves toward restarting U.S.-DPRK dialogue in late summer and early fall 2002 were dramatically derailed by the "Kelly revelations" of October. On October 16th, the U.S. State Department announced that, some eleven days earlier, Assistant Secretary of State James A. Kelly had confronted his counterparts in Pyongyang with evidence that North Korea had "a program to enrich uranium for nuclear weapons, in violation of the Agreed Framework and other agreements."[40] According to U.S. accounts (North Korea publicly neither confirmed nor denied the accusation), the DPRK officials acknowledged the existence of this program and declared the Agreed Framework "nullified." But North Korea insisted that the United States was to blame for the failure of the Agreed Framework, and offered to enter a new set of talks to resolve the crisis. The United States repeatedly refused to negotiate with North Korea before Pyongyang ceased all of its nuclear-related activities, and in November Washington suspended deliveries of fuel oil to North Korea required under the Agreed Framework. This was followed by a rapidly escalating set of moves on the part of North Korea toward restarting its plutonium program, frozen by the 1994 Agreement: Pyongyang announced its intention to reopen its nuclear power plant at Yŏngbyŏn, expelled International Atomic Energy Agency (IAEA) inspectors at the end of December 2002, announced its withdrawal from the Non-Proliferation Treaty (NPT) in January 2003, and began to remove spent nuclear fuel rods from storage in February—the latter an act that had brought the United States and North Korea to the brink of war in 1994.

While the crisis in U.S.-DPRK relations deepened in 2003, North-South relations continued to move forward. Indeed, a distinctive aspect of the 2002–2003 crisis was the common ground Pyongyang could find with the Seoul government in criticizing the American approach to Korea. This was the reverse of the 1993–1994 crisis, in which the ROK government of Kim Young Sam deeply feared U.S.-DPRK "collusion" at the expense of South Korea's national interest. This is not to say that Seoul-Pyongyang relations became cordial or that Seoul suddenly broke its ties with Washington; Seoul decried North Korea's development of nuclear weapons, for example, and Pyongyang attacked the Roh Moo Hyun government for agreeing to send South Korean troops to Iraq.[41] Roh visited Washington in May, and he and President Bush tried to put a unified face on their policy toward North Korea; Pyongyang condemned the Roh-Bush joint statement as "a perfidious act which runs counter to the basic spirit of the June 15 North-South Declaration."[42] But various agreements and meetings between the ROK and DPRK went ahead despite the new nuclear crisis, including a seven-point agreement on inter-Korean economic relations, signed by the representatives of North and South Korea in Pyongyang in late May. The two sides agreed on the establishment of a special Industrial Zone in the North Korean city of Kaesŏng, reconnection of east and west coast railway lines, and other joint projects.[43] For its part, the United States proposed a multilateral forum to resolve the new nuclear issue, a six-way dialogue among North and

Figure 5.1
The six-party talks.

South Korea, China, Russia, Japan, and the United States. The six-party talks began in Beijing in April 2003 (Figure 5.1).

In the midst of this impasse in U.S.-North Korean relations, George W. Bush was elected to a second term as U.S. President. North Korea seemed to find the second Bush administration just as hostile as the first, if not more so. Pyongyang seized upon Condoleezza Rice's reference to North Korea as an "outpost of tyranny" in her inauguration speech as the new Secretary of State, claiming that this and other statements proved that the "true intention of the second-term Bush administration is not only to further its policy to isolate and stifle the DPRK pursued by the first-term office but to escalate it." On 10 February, 2005, the DPRK Foreign Ministry confirmed that North Korea had "manufactured nukes" and was now a "nuclear weapons state." Nevertheless, North Korea insisted that nuclear weapons were purely for self-defense against a hostile United States, and the official Korea Central News Agency reiterated that "[t]he DPRK's principled stand to solve the issue through dialogue and negotiations and its ultimate goal to denuclearize the Korean Peninsula remains unchanged."[44] In the meantime, until U.S. attitudes and policy toward North Korea shifted to one of peaceful coexistence, the nuclear issue could not be resolved and North Korea would stay out of the Six-Party Talks.[45] North Korea thus blamed the United States for the suspension of the Six-Party Talks, but left the door open for their resumption.

There were, however, indications that the second Bush administration, unlike the first, was serious about negotiating with the North Koreans. Christopher Hill, a career diplomat who had been a key negotiator for the Balkan crisis under Clinton, was appointed ambassador to Seoul and then, less than a year later, chief U.S. representative to the Six-Party Talks. While the United States engaged in official dialogue with North Korea in Beijing, a team led by Ambassador Joseph DeTrani pursued "informal" dialogue with North

Korean representatives in New York. This helped to get the Six-Party Process back on track. In June 2005, the movement toward renewed U.S.-DPRK formal dialogue rapidly picked up momentum. On June 10, President Bush met with ROK President Roh Moo Hyun in Washington. On June 17, as part of a South Korean delegation visiting Pyongyang for the fifth anniversary of the June 15 North-South Summit, ROK Unification Minister Chung Dong Young met with Kim Jong Il, and Kim conveyed to him North Korea's desire to return to the Six-Party Talks by the end of July. Later, Minister Chung explained that South Korea had promised to supply electricity to the North in order to help resolve the nuclear issue, as North Korea had long insisted that its nuclear program was primarily intended to alleviate its severe energy shortages.[46] Finally, on July 10, North Korea announced that it would return to the talks. Secretary Rice insisted that the U.S. position had not changed: "We are not talking about enhancement of the current proposal," that is, the proposal of June 2004.[47]

During the thirteen months the talks had been suspended, both the United States and North Korea insisted they would not move from their respective positions. But a close reading of each side's rhetoric and actions during that time suggested otherwise. North Korea had begun to speak of "peaceful coexistence" rather than outright normalization or a peace agreement in the immediate future; the United States referred to North Korea's "sovereignty" and quietly pursued bilateral discussions with the DPRK both in New York and Beijing. As the talks began on July 25, North Korean and American diplomats met in Beijing for extensive one-on-one discussions, despite the longstanding U.S. resistance to bilateral talks. Ambassador Hill described a step-by-step process of each side working simultaneously to resolve the nuclear standoff, rather than North Korea conceding everything up front; he described this as "words for words and actions for actions," exactly the phrase the North Koreans had long used. Hill's North Korean counterpart, chief negotiator Kim Kye Gwan, opened his remarks with a more conciliatory, less belligerent tone than earlier North Korean statements.[48] When the six parties met for a fourth round of talks in September, they produced for the first time a joint statement on the denuclearization of the Korean peninsula.[49] The six-point statement was notable for its vagueness; issues of procedure, much less implementation, were far from resolved, and little progress was made toward resolution in the fifth round, held in early November.[50] Nevertheless, the very existence of such talks signified a considerable improvement in U.S.-North Korean relations since the tense days of late 2002 and early 2003, when—as in the 1993–1994 crisis—the two seemed on the verge of military confrontation. As the world's sole superpower and the most important external presence on the Korean peninsula, the United States was an essential factor in any resolution of the inter-Korean conflict. North-South Korean relations could not proceed very far without U.S. cooperation and encouragement. Despite important differences, by the end of 2005, after three years of growing divergence, the United States and South Korea were again converging on how to approach North Korea. If anything, the United States had shifted toward Seoul's position of negotiation and dialogue, and away from a policy of confrontation and coercion. Perhaps, with the United States and South Korea reasonably in sync, North-South reconciliation could proceed apace.

THE TWO KOREAS IN THE WORLD

More than sixty years after American policy planners drew an imaginary line across the middle of the Korean peninsula to expedite the Japanese surrender, Korea remains divided. The Americans and Soviets who liberated Korea in 1945 could not possibly have foreseen the suffering and destruction that would follow from this division. But even after one of the major powers who oversaw this division has long disappeared, after the Cold War that solidified Korean division has entered the dustbin of history, the two Korean regimes remain in place. Korea's continued division has its own perverse dynamic, both within the peninsula and in connection to regional and global forces, which go well beyond the World War II settlement and Cold War confrontation that made division possible. The implacable hostility between the two Koreas is less a product of the Cold War than of the brutal, fratricidal "hot war" that took place in the 1950s. The two Germanies did not fight a war with each other, and even so unification was far from a smooth process. The two Koreas, blood brothers and at the same time blood enemies, have just begun to reach the degree of tentative cooperation achieved between East and West Germany in the 1970s. Reconciliation, much less peaceful unification, remains a distant dream.

Another reason for the persistent division of Korea is that North Korea simply refuses to disappear. East Germany was, and remained for its entire existence, a Soviet creature propped up by Moscow's army. When the USSR withdrew its support, collapse soon followed. North Korea, on the other hand, was far more independent than the Soviet leadership would have preferred and remained independent long after the Soviet Union itself disintegrated. Nor is China able to affect North Korean behavior to any great extent, despite being North Korea's only remaining major ally and largest source of food and energy aid. For all its unsavory aspects, the North Korean regime was built upon a nationalist basis that gave it a far greater degree of domestic legitimacy than the Soviet "satellites" in Eastern Europe and Mongolia, and has been fiercely determined to follow its own path of self-determination, if not literal self-reliance. North Korea is in no position to conquer the South by force today, as it attempted to do in 1950, but neither is it willing to compromise its own sovereignty and military defense. Nor is South Korea willing to risk devastation on the peninsula by attempting to conquer the North. The standoff continues.

The regional and global dynamics regarding Korea have also not been entirely conducive to unification, certainly not peaceful unification in the near term. None of the major powers with a stake in the Korean problem—China, Russia, Japan, and the United States—is willing to risk unification through a renewed war on the peninsula or the violent collapse of North Korea (although the United States may be a partial exception to this). On the other hand, the surrounding powers are also wary of any sudden change in the status quo. China is leery of a potentially pro-U.S. unified Korea under South Korean auspices, and this inhibits the degree of pressure it is willing to put on the North to change. The United States is very reluctant to give concessions to North Korea, which American leaders (especially in the Republican party) consider "appeasement." Russia and Japan have much less influence on Korean affairs, and it is arguable that Japan, at least, prefers the status quo of a divided Korea than the challenge of an assertive and nationalistic unified Korea. Thus, by default if nothing else, Korea's neighboring countries, including the United States, have moved toward the acceptance (again, with the partial exception of the United States) of a gradually and peacefully integrated Korean peninsula rather than a sudden or violent unification.

Inter-Korean relations have come a long way since the existential antagonism of the early Cold War. At the present time, neither North nor South Korea speaks much of unification in the near future, or of the eradication of the other Korean regime. Since the June 2000 summit, both sides have acknowledged that unification is likely to be a long, gradual process that must be preceded by a prolonged period of co-existence and cooperation. In part, this change in attitude derives from the "lessons" of German unification. For South Korea, which is in a much weaker position economically than West Germany was for absorbing its communist sister state, sudden unification would be enormously expensive and disruptive, with the potential to reverse decades of hard-earned economic growth. For the leaders of North Korea, a German-style absorption by the South would mean the end of their system and their privileged position in it, not to mention possible prosecution for war crimes. Under these circumstances, it is highly unlikely that the North Korean regime would give up without a fight, which could have devastating consequences for the entire region. No outside party is willing to provoke North Korea to collapse while its leaders refuse to go quietly into the night.

The Korean peninsula, including North Korea, has not escaped the forces of globalization that so deeply affect the world in the early twenty-first century. North Korea has

Figure 5.2
Kim Jong Il and Kim Dae Jung from their 2000 summit meeting in Pyongyang.

attempted to limit and control these forces as much as possible, perhaps more than any other industrial state in modern times. Yet, economic and cultural changes are entering the North, in part as a result of greater interaction with the South. The DMZ is no longer the impenetrable boundary it was only a decade ago, as hundreds of South Koreans cross into the North every day for business and tourism. South Korean joint ventures in the North remain for the most part small-scale concerns, and few have made a profit. But this economic presence, along with that of Chinese, Japanese, and Western businesses in the North, is a new development with potentially far-reaching consequences for the future of North Korea and of Korean integration.

For inter-Korean relations to move beyond this still-limited interaction to genuine integration, both sides need to re-examine the deep-rooted mutual distrust on which their respective states have been legitimized. Economic ties alone will not eliminate the animosity between the two Koreas, unless they are accompanied by a change in cultural attitudes toward acceptance of the deep and long-term differences that have developed between the two Korean populations.[51] Korea is still a divided nation, but not a "divided nation in a divided world," as it was during the Cold War.[52] Korean division has become internalized—within the Korean peninsula, within each Korea, and in the mentalities of individual Koreans. After sixty years of division, Korea is not—if it ever was—a homogenous society. Only an appreciation of difference will allow the two Koreas genuinely to become one.

Six

One Korea, Many Koreas

What is Korea? Who are Koreans? The answers to these questions are not as straightforward as they may seem. At a minimum, Korea is one nation, two states, and many communities beyond the Korean peninsula. Each Korean state claims to represent the whole Korean people, but the authority of each state ends sharply at the DMZ, and only illegally and at great personal risk can a resident of one Korean state move to the other. According to the laws of both regimes, all people within the boundaries of the Korean states are Koreans—except those who are not, including resident foreigners both legal and illegal. Then again, among resident foreigners, people of Korean descent from places such as China, Russia, and the United States may consider themselves Korean, except that legally they are not citizens of the Korean state in which they reside (meaning, usually, the Republic of Korea in the South). The descendents of those who left the Korean peninsula to settle abroad may feel a sense of kinship and emotional attachment to their ancestral land, but if they are not citizens of the ROK or DPRK, neither state has authority over them. On the other hand, hundreds of thousands of people migrated from China to Korea in the late nineteenth and early twentieth centuries, yet even those born in Korea are rarely Korean citizens, and their numbers have steadily dwindled since the 1940s.[1]

Governments of some kind have existed for millennia, bonds of kinship and community even longer, but the nation-state is a product of modern history going back little more than 200 years in Europe, and in the rest of the world considerably less.[2] Combining sovereign political authority, territorial integrity, and a strong sentiment of belonging (power, place, and identity), the nation-state became the universal form of social organization with modern globalization in the nineteenth and twentieth centuries, reaching its apex in the wave of decolonization in the two decades after World War II. At the beginning of this period, the kingdom of Chosŏn began to move toward the nation-state ideal—or at least, Korean intellectuals like the great historian Sin Ch'ae-ho first imagined Korea to be a nation, one consisting of a single Korean ethnicity (minjok).[3] But the Korean nation-state was imagined at the very moment of its impossibility. *There has never been a modern, unitary, independent Korean nation-state.* The Korean nation has been, and remains, a nation in fragments.[4] Foreign domination, colonization, national division, and diaspora characterize Korea's entire "long twentieth century" from the late nineteenth century to the present.

In this regard, Korea is not so much a unique victim of modernity as a striking example of the paradox of national identity in a global age. The twentieth century was one of both homogenization and fragmentation, alternatively and often at the same time.[5] Nationalism, the emotional and political expression of the desire for national independence and unity, emerged in Korea as elsewhere as a form of resistance to external domination. Koreans have long imagined themselves to be one people, speaking a single language and sharing a common culture. Few places have emphasized unity as much as modern Korea, from Syngman Rhee's slogan of "One People's Principle" (Ilminjuŭi, derived or distilled from Chinese nationalist leader Sun Yat-sen's "Three People's Principles" or Sanminzhuyi), to South Korean President Chun Doo Hwan's secret "Society of One" (Hanahoe), to Korea's most successful religious export, Reverend Sun-myung Moon's "Unification Church" (T'ongilgyo). Yet this stress on unity has belied, or perhaps attempts to compensate for, a reality of division, diversity, and difference.

Most obviously, the division of Korea into two mutually exclusive regimes, each claiming to represent the people of the entire peninsula, contradicts the idea of Korean unity. But division also reinforces unity as an ideal: the abstract goal of political unification elides both the real differences that have emerged between the two societies since division, and the differences within each of them. It almost goes without saying that after sixty years of radically different political, economic, and social systems, the two Koreas have evolved into two very different kinds of societies. But even within South Korea, for example, regional diversity and "regionalism" (what Koreans call "regional sentiment" or chibang kamchŏng) is a powerful force in interpersonal relations, economic activity, and politics. While some of this regionalism may have ancient roots, it is mostly a product of recent history, and in particular the political and economic favoritism showed to the southeastern Kyŏngsang area (and conversely, discrimination toward the southwestern Ch'ŏlla region) since the 1960s.[6] Presidents from Park Chung Hee in 1963 to Kim Young Sam in 1992 came from Kyŏngsang, Kim Dae Jung and his followers from Ch'ŏlla. Despite attempts to level the playing field since the Kim Dae Jung administration, regionalism has been a determining factor for political identification, and a key cleavage in South Korean society, until the present. Little is known of regionalism in North Korea, but some form of it no doubt exists there as well.

Even if we acknowledge that people who can trace their ancestry on the Korean peninsula far back in history are all "Koreans," belonging to a single ethnicity, a growing number of people in South Korea are not Korean in this sense. One by-product of South Korea's economic success is the influx of workers, most illegal, from other parts of Asia and beyond. Almost nonexistent in the 1970s, by the 1990s such workers numbered in the hundreds of thousands.[7] There are few legal, cultural, or social service facilities in South Korea geared to such "non-Korean" residents, and only in very recent years has the South Korean government attempted to deal with this problem. Some of the more progressive nongovernmental organizations have taken up the cause of foreign workers' rights as well. Still, a society educated to believe in its homogeneity will not find it easy to absorb a growing population of workers who are often visibly, and certainly culturally, "different." Under these circumstances, such people can hardly expect to be accepted as Korean, unless the definition of "Korean" itself changes.

The contradiction between the ideology of sameness and the reality of difference is nowhere more evident than in the treatment of North Korean refugees in South Korea. The ROK has long claimed to welcome defectors from the North, but until recently this policy rarely needed to be tested in practice: there were very few such defectors. The numbers are still relatively small, less than ten thousand in a population of nearly fifty million, but even so the North Korean refugees in the South by and large have had a very difficult time adjusting to South Korean society. This is not only because of the problem of adjusting to life under capitalism after growing up under socialism, a problem common to all defectors across the erstwhile "Iron Curtain" as well as in postcommunist Europe. It is also because, defectors consistently report, former North Koreans feel a strong sense of discrimination and condescension from their South Korean hosts, who treat them as ignorant country bumpkins and have little patience or tolerance for their lack of familiarity with the workings of South Korean society.[8] If South Korea has difficulty absorbing a few thousand refugees from the North, one can only imagine the enormous social and cultural problems that a sudden unification would produce, especially if it came after a collapse of the North Korean political system and its absorption into the South. As the anthropologist Richard Grinker has argued, any serious consideration of the consequences of unification must recognize the need to change popular attitudes toward North Koreans, and to stress the need to accept difference.[9] Otherwise, the frictions between former North Koreans and South Koreans in a unified Korea could be profound, far worse even than the problems between Easterners and Westerners in postunification Germany.

There are some indications that South Korea may be already becoming a more tolerant society, helped by the democratization of recent years. Democratization itself is still incomplete, according to many South Korean critics, beset by regionalism and personalism, manipulated by the old elites. Professor Choi Jang-jip of Korea University, one of South Korea's most distinguished political scientists, argues that democracy has deteriorated considerably since the euphoria of the late 1980s, retaining its procedural form but losing its ability to express the interests of society as a whole, having been co-opted by the forces of conservatism.[10] Nevertheless, democracy has the potential at least to articulate a new, less ethnically based nationalism and move Korea toward a more pluralistic civic nationalism. This can only happen with the full participation of civil society and the input of regional, social, gender, and ethnic strata that have traditionally been marginalized in Korean politics. A more tolerant and inclusive politics is important not just for South Korea itself, but in order to reduce the potential for social conflict in a Korea that is unified in the future.

The issue of unification has been manipulated by political elites North and South, and Koreans (especially in the South) have been sobered by the potential costs of unification in recent years, but nevertheless overcoming Korea's division is the genuine hope of the vast majority of Koreans. Modern Korea could have faced many problems of its own making, including war and mass violence, but national division was an utterly unnatural product of foreign intervention and the arbitrary decisions of outside powers. Divided Korea was the result of the geopolitics of an earlier age of globalization, an age that has long since passed. North Korea adapted itself to the challenges of the post-World War II global order in its own idiosyncratic fashion and did rather well economically, until it reached the limits of its self-reliant system and found itself unable to adjust successfully to the changing regional and global environment. South Korea did much better than the North after the mid-1970s, and despite the setback of the 1997 financial crisis, had positioned itself as a significant player in the global economy by the end of the twentieth century. But South Korea too remains inhibited by the problem of national division and the constant insecurity of military tension on the peninsula. A politically unified peninsula, freed from the constraints of the current military face-off, could be a much more significant actor in a more integrated region and world. Unified Korea would remain diverse, as Korea has always been, but that diversity would be contained within an essential unity. Korea is one, and it is also many.

NOTES

CHAPTER ONE

1. H.B. Drake, *Korea of the Japanese* (London: John Lane, 1930), p. 3.
2. Michael M. Weinstein, ed., *Globalization: What's New?* (New York: Columbia University Press, 2005).
3. See Samuel S. Kim, ed., *Korea's Globalization* (New York: Cambridge University Press, 2000).
4. David Held, et al., *Global Transformations: Politics, Economics and Culture* (Stanford, CA: Stanford University Press, 1995).
5. Marcus Noland, *Avoiding the Apocalypse: The Future of the Two Koreas* (Washington, DC: Institute for International Economics, 2000), pp. 59–60.
6. Don Oberdorfer, *The Two Koreas: A Contemporary History* (Reading, MA: Addison-Wesley, 1997), p. 3. For an insightful critique of the "invasion hypothesis" in Korean historiography, see Hyung Il Pai, "The Politics of Korea's Past: The Legacy of Japanese Colonial Archeology in the Korean Peninsula," *East Asian History*, no. 7 (June 1994), and idem, Constructing "Korean" Origins: *A Critical Review of Archaeology, Historiography, and Racial Myth in Korean State-Formation Theories* (Cambridge, MA: Harvard University East Asia Series, 2000).
7. Martin W. Lewis and Karin Wigen, *The Myth of Continents: A Critique of Metageography* (Berkeley, CA: University of California Press, 1997).
8. Peter Duus, *The Abacus and the Sword: The Japanese Penetration of Korea, 1895–1910* (Berkeley, CA: University of California Press, 1995), p. 49.

9. On the rise of geopolitical thinking in the nineteenth and twentieth centuries, see Gearoid O Tuathail, *Critical Geopolitics: The Politics of Writing Global Space* (Minneapolis, MN: University of Minnesota Press, 1996). The best account of Korea in late nineteenth-century geopolitics is George Alexander Lensen, *Balance of Intrigue: International Rivalry in Korea and Manchuria, 1884–1899* (Tallahassee, FL: University Press of Florida, 1982).

10. John B. Duncan, *Origins of the Chosŏn Dynasty* (Seattle, WA: University of Washington Press, 2000).

11. James Palais, *Politics and Policy in Traditional Korea* (Cambridge, MA: Harvard University Press, 1975).

12. Gari Ledyard, *The Dutch Come to Korea* (Seoul: Royal Asiatic Society, Korea Branch, 1971).

13. James Palais, *Confucian Statecraft and Korean Institutions: Yu Hyŏngwŏn and the late Chosŏn Dynasty* (Seattle, WA: University of Washington Press, 1996).

14. Gi-wook Shin and Michael Robinson, eds., *Colonial Modernity in Korea* (Cambridge, MA: Harvard University Asia Center, 1999).

15. John Merrill, *Korea: The Peninsular Origins of the War* (Newark, DE: University of Delaware Press, 1989).

16. Alexandre Y. Mansourov, "Communist War Coalition Formation and the Origins of the Korean War." Ph.D. dissertation, Columbia University, 1997.

17. Barry K. Gills, *Korea versus Korea: A Case of Contested Legitimacy* (London: Routledge, 1996).

18. Gregory Henderson et al., eds., *Divided Nations in a Divided World* (New York: D. McKay Co., 1974).

CHAPTER TWO

1. David I. Steinberg, "Burma/Myanmar: Under the Military," in James W. Morley, ed., *Driven by Growth: Political Change in the Asia-Pacific Region* (Armonk, NY: M.E. Sharpe, revised ed. 1999), pp. 35–37.

2. Chalmers Johnson, *Blowback: The Costs and Consequences of American Empire* (New York: Henry Holt & Co., 2000), p. 102.

3. Jung-en Woo, *Race to the Swift: State and Finance in Korean Industrialization* (New York: Columbia University Press, 1991), p. 45.

4. Ch'oe Hae-wol, "The Character of the Anti-National University Movement during the US Military Government." *Yŏksa pip'yong* no. 1 (Summer 1988), pp. 6–30.

5. Charles K. Armstrong, "The Cultural Cold War in Korea," *Journal of Asian Studies* vol. 62, no. 1 (February 2003), pp. 71–100.

6. Gi-wook Shin, "South Korean Anti-Americanism: A Comparative Perspective," *Asian Survey* vol. 36, no. 3 (August 1996), pp. 787–803.

7. David I. Steinberg, ed., *Korean Attitudes Toward the United States: Changing Dynamics* (Armonk, NY: M.E. Sharpe, 2004).

8. Suh-kyung Yoon, "Swept Up on a Wave," *Far Eastern Economic Review,* 18 October 2001. http://www.feer.com.

9. Anthony Leung, *Korean Cinema: The New Hong Kong* (London: Trafford, 2003).

10. A December 2002 poll by the Joongang Ilbo newspaper showed that 36 percent of South Koreans viewed the United States unfavorably, only 13 percent favorably and 50 percent were neutral. Only among those over age 50 did a majority view the United States favorably.

11. Katharine H.S. Moon, "Nationalism, Anti-Americanism, and Democratic Consolidation," in Samuel S. Kim, ed., *Korea's Democratization* (Cambridge, UK: Cambridge University Press, 2003), pp. 154–155.

12. Meredith Woo-Cumings, ed., *The Developmental State* (Ithaca, NY: Cornell University Press, 1999).

13. Eun Mee Kim, *Big Business, Strong State: Collusion and Conflict in South Korean Development, 1960–1990* (Albany, NY: State University of New York Press, 1997).

14. Barry K. Gills, "Economic Liberalization and Reform in South Korea in the 1990s: A 'Coming of Age' or a Case of 'Graduation Blues?'" *Third World Quarterly* vol. 17, no. 4 (Autumn 1996), pp. 667–688.

15. James Palais, *Politics and Policy in Traditional Korea* (Cambridge, MA: Harvard University Press, 1975), pp. 4–5, 58.

16. Carter J. Eckert, *Offspring of Empire: The Koch'ang Kims and the Colonial Origins of Korean Capitalism, 1876–1945* (Seattle, WA: University of Washington Press, 1991).

17. Publicly, Park referred not to wartime Japan or colonial Korea as his model, but to Japan's Meiji Restoration of 1868. See Park Chung Hee, *The Country, the Revolution, and I* (Seoul: Hollym, 1970 [1963]).

18. George E. Ogle, *South Korea: Dissent within the Economic Miracle* (London: Zed Books, 1990).

19. Frank Baldwin, "America's Rented Troops: South Koreans in Vietnam," *Bulletin of Concerned Asian Scholars* vol. 8, no. 1 (January 1976), pp. 37–38.

20. Woo, *Race to the Swift*, p. 95.

21. Alice Amsden, *Asia's Next Giant: South Korea and Late Industrialization* (Oxford, UK: Oxford University Press, 1989), p. 23.

22. Bruce Cumings, "The Origins and Development of the Northeast Asian Political Economy: Industrial Sectors, Product Cycles and Political Consequences," *International Organization* vol. 38, no. 1 (Winter 1984), pp. 1–40.

23. Amsden, *Asia's Next Giant*, p. 152.

24. Amsden, *Asia's Next Giant*, p. 48; Linsu Kim, *Imitation to Innovation: The Dynamics of Korea's Technological Learning* (Boston, MA: Harvard Business School Press, 1997), p. 1.

25. Kim, *Big Business, Strong State*, p. 200.

26. For the IMF's own account of the crisis and the IMF's response, see http://www.imf.org/external/np/exr/facts/asia.htm.

27. Joseph Stiglitz, *Globalization and its Discontents* (New York: Norton, 2002), p. 27.

28. Cited in Korea Economic Institute, "South Korean Economic Data," August 2005. http://www.keia.org.

29. Pamela Licalzi O'Connell, "Korea's High-Tech Utopia, Where Everything is Observed," *New York Times*, October 5, 2005, p. 6.

30. At the end of 1905 Tonghak was renamed Ch'ŏndogyo (Teaching of the Heavenly Way), and became a major advocate of Korean independence during the colonial period. See Benjamin Weems, *Reform, Rebellion, and the Heavenly Way* (Tucson, AZ: University of Arizona Press, 1964).

31. Vipan Chandra, *Imperialism, Resistance, and Reform in Late Nineteenth-Century Korea: Enlightenment and the Independence Club* (Berkeley, CA: Institute of East Asian Studies, University of California, Berkeley, Center for Korean Studies, 1988).

32. Among the best accounts of the Kwangju Massacre are Lee Jai-eui, *Kwangju Diary: Beyond Death, Beyond the Darkness of the Age* trans. Kap Su Seol and Nick Mamatas (Los Angeles, CA: UCLA Asia Pacific Monograph Series, 1999); Henry Scott-Stokes and Lee Jai-eui, eds., *The Kwangju Uprising: Eyewitness Press Accounts of Korea's Tiananmen* (Armonk, NY: M.E. Sharpe, 2000); and Gi-wook Shin and Kyung Moon Hwang, eds., *Contentious Kwangju: The May 18th Uprising in Korea's Past and Present* (Lanham, MD: Rowman & Littlefield, 2003).

33. Park Chung Hee, *How to Build a Nation* (1971). Cited in Yongho Ch'oe, Peter H. Lee and Wm. Theodore de Bary, eds., *Source of Korean Tradition, vol. 2: From the Sixteenth to the Twentieth Centuries* (New York: Columbia University Press, 2000), p. 396.

34. Doowon Suh, "From Individual Welfare to Social Change: The Expanding Goals of Korean White-Collar Labor Unions, 1987–1995," Ph.D. Dissertation, University of Chicago, 1998.

35. Hagen Koo, *Korean Workers: The Culture and Politics of Class Formation* (Ithaca, NY: Cornell University Press, 2001), p. 18.

36. Kenneth Wells, ed., *South Korea's Minjung Movement: The Culture and Politics of Dissidence* (Honolulu: University of Hawaii Press, 1995).

37. Koo, *Korean Workers*, p. 159.

38. Don Oberdorfer, *The Two Koreas: A Contemporary History* (Reading, MA: Basic Books, 1997), p. 166.

39. Sunhyuk Kim, *The Politics of Democratization in Korea: The Role of Civil Society* (Pittsburgh, PA: University of Pittsburgh Press, 2000).

40. David Scofield, "The Dawning of Pluralism in South Korea," *Asia Times*, March 30, 2004. http://www.atimes.com.

41. Sallie W. Yea, "Regionalism and Political-Economic Differentiation in Korean Development: Power Maintenance and the State as Hegemonic Power Bloc," *Korea Journal* vol. 34, no. 2 (Summer 1994), pp. 5–29.

42. Joongang Ilbo, October 14, 2004.

43. Chang, Kyung-Sup. "Compressed Modernity and its Discontents: South Korean Society in Transition," *Economy and Society* vol. 28, no. 1 (1999), pp. 30–55.

44. Laura C. Nelson, *Measured Excess: Status, Gender and Consumer Nationalism in South Korea* (New York: Columbia University Press, 2000), pp. 107–136.

45. Lee Hyo-sik, "One in Four Rural Bachelors Marry Foreigners," *The Korea Times*, June 27, 2005. http://times.hankooki.com. Of these foreign women, the vast majority (over 90 percent) were from eastern Asia, the largest group being ethnic Koreans from China, followed by Vietnamese and Filipinas.

46. Jung Sun Park, "The Korean Wave: Transnational Cultural Flows in East Asia," in Charles K. Armstrong, *Korea at the Center: Dynamics of Regionalism in Northeast Asia* (Armonk, NY: M.E. Sharpe, 2006), pp. 257–262.

47. The ROK Ministry of Tourism jumped aboard the Korean Wave and made it their major focus of tourism promotion in Asia. See http://www.knto.or.kr/eng/hallyu/hallyu.html.

48. Paek Wŏn-dam, *Hallyu: Tong Asia ŭi Munhwa Sŏnt'aek* [The Korean Wave: East Asia's Cultural Choice] (Seoul: Pentagram, 2005).

49. Roh Moo-hyun, "A New Takeoff Toward an Age of Peace and Prosperity," http://www.icasinc.org/2003/2003l/2003lrmh.html.

50. Bruce Klingner, "China Shock for South Korea," *Asia Times*, September 11, 2004. http://www.atimes.com/atimes/Korea/FI11Dg03.html.

51. Joint Statement of the Fourth Round of the Six-Party Talks, Beijing, September 19, 2005. http://www.state.gov/r/pa/prs/ps/2005/53490.htm.

CHAPTER THREE

1. Such a reading of sadae goes back to the pioneering historian Shin Ch'ae-ho in the early twentieth century. See Michael Robinson, "National Identity and the Thought of Shin Ch'ae-ho: Sadaejuŭi and Chuch'e in History and Politics," *Journal of Korean Studies* no. 5 (1984), and Andre Schmid, *Korea between Empires, 1895–1919* (New York: Columbia University Press, 2002).

2. Juche has been elaborated into a "philosophy" in numerous North Korean texts. See for example Ko Rim, *Chuch'e ch'ŏrhak immun* [Introduction to Juche Philosophy] (n.p., 1988), and Kim Jong Il, *Chuch'e ch'ŏrhak e taehayo* [On Juche Philosophy] (Pyongyang: Chosŏn Nodongdang Ch'ulp'ansa, 2000).

3. Bruce Cumings, "Corporatism in North Korea," *Journal of Korean Studies* no. 4 (1982–1983).

4. Charles K. Armstrong, *The North Korean Revolution, 1945–1950* (Ithaca, NY: Cornell University Press, 2003).

5. *Postwar Rehabilitation and Development of the National Economy* (Pyongyang: Foreign Languages Publishing House, 1957), p. 8.

6. Kang Chŏng-gu, "The Korean War and the Construction of Socialism in North Korea," *Hanguk kwa kukje chongch'i* [Korea and International Politics] vol. 6, no. 2 (Autumn 1990), pp. 95–137.

7. Kim Il Sung, *On the Building of the Worker's Party of Korea*, vol. 2 (Pyongyang: Foreign Languages Publishing House, 1978), pp. 233–234.

8. Dae-Sook Suh, *Kim Il Sung, the North Korean leader* (New York: Columbia University Press, 1988), pp. 130–134; Koon Woo Nam, *The North Korean Communist Leadership, 1945–1965: A study of Factionalism and Political Consolidation* (Tuscaloosa, AL: University of Alabama Press, 1974), pp. 92–95.

9. Andrei Lankov, *Crisis in North Korea: The Failure of De-Stalinization, 1956* (Honolulu: University of Hawaii Press, 2005).

10. Lim Un, *The Founding of a Dynasty in North Korea: An Authentic Biography of Kim Il Sung* (Tokyo: Jiyu-sha, 1982), chapter 6. "Lim Un" is a pseudonym for Ho Chin, a North Korean exile residing in the former Soviet Union.

11. Nam, *North Korean Communist Leadership*, p. 116.

12. Glenn D. Paige and Dong Jun Lee, "The Post-War Politics of North Korea," in Robert A. Scalapino, ed., *North Korea Today* (New York: Praeger, 1963), p. 19.

13. Glenn D. Paige, "North Korea and the Emulation of Russian and Chinese Behavior," in A. Doak Barnett, ed., *Communist Strategies in Asia: A Comparative Analysis of Governments and Parties* (New York: Praeger, 1963).

14. Kim Il Sung, "Everything for the Postwar Rehabilitation and Development of the National Economy," *Works* vol. 8, p. 15.

15. For a comparison between the two economies, see United States Central Intelligence Agency, *Korea: The Economic Race between the North and the South* (Washington, D.C.: Government Printing Office, 1978).

16. Cited in Ellen Brun and Jacques Hersh, *Socialist Korea: A Case Study of the Strategy of Economic Development* (New York: Monthly Review Press, 1976), p. 165.

17. Chung, *North Korean Economy*, p. 10.

18. Lee, *Rural North Korea*, p. 27.

19. The North Korean cooperative movement was likely influenced by the People's Commune campaign being launched simultaneously in China, especially in the second stage of amalgamation. However, the DPRK had begun the formation of large cooperatives well before the commune movement, and did not simply copy the Chinese model, as some observers have suggested. See Chong-Sik Lee, "Land Reform, Collectivisation and the Peasants in North Korea," *China Quarterly* no. 4 (April–June 1963), p. 76.

20. Chung, *North Korean Economy*, p. 60.

21. Chung, *North Korean Economy*, p. 62.

22. Paige, "Emulation," p. 242.

23. Ryu Kiljae, "The 'Ch'ŏllima Movement' and Socialist Economic Construction Campaigns: Focusing on Comparison to the Stakhonovite Movement and the 'Great Leap Forward'," in Ch'oe Ch'ŏngho et al., *Pukhan sahoejuŭi kŏnsŏl ui chŏngch'i kyongje* [The Political Economy of North Korean Socialist Construction] (Seoul: Kyungnam University Far East Institute, 1993), p. 75. The 1972 Constitution referred to the Ch'ŏllima Movement as the "general line [ch'ong nosŏn] of socialist construction in the DPRK."

24. Scalapino and Lee, *Communism in Korea*, p. 540.

25. Scalapino and Lee, *Communism in Korea*, p. 575.

26. Brun and Hersh, *Socialist Korea*, p. 187.

27. See Chŏng Sang-hun (Joseph S. Chung), "Agricultural and Industrial Management Systems: Ch'ŏngsalli Method and Taean Work System," in Ch'oe, *Pukhan sahoejuŭi kŏnsŏl*, pp. 81–104.

28. Ilpyong J. Kim, *Communist Politics in North Korea* (New York: Praeger, 1975), pp. 85–86.

29. Kim Il Sung, "On Eliminating Formalism and Establishing Juche [chuch'e] in Ideological Work," *Works* vol. 9, pp. 395–417.

30. Pak Hyong-jung, *Pukhanjŏk hyŏnsang ŭi yŏn'gu: Pukhan sahoejuŭi kŏnsŏl ŭi chŏngch'i kyŏngjehak* [The North Korean Phenomenon: The Political Economy of North Korea's Socialist Construction] (Seoul: Yongusa, 1994), p. 172.

31. Kim, "On Eliminating Dogmatism and Formalism," p. 396.

32. Kim Il Sung, *On Juche in our Revolution* (Pyongyang: Foreign Languages Publishing House, 1977), pp. 428–429.

33. Chung, *North Korean Economy*, p. 99.

34. Byung Chol Koh, *The Foreign Policy Systems of North and South Korea* (Berkeley, CA: University of California Press, 1984), p. 59.

35. Kim, *Communist Politics*, p. 87.

36. Scalapino and Lee, *Communism in Korea*, p. 617.

37. Tai-sung An, *North Korea in Transition: From Dictatorship to Dynasty* (Westport, CT: Greenwood Press, 1983), pp. 86, 93.

38. Ralph N. Clough, *Embattled Korea: The Rivalry for International Support* (Boulder, CO: Westview Press, 1987), p. 87.

39. Clough, *Embattled Korea*, p. 50.

40. Chin O. Chung, *P'yongyang between Peking and Moscow: North Korea's Involvement in the Sino-Soviet Dispute, 1958–1975* (Tuscaloosa, AL: University of Alabama Press, 1978), pp. 55–57.

41. Chung, *P'yongyang Between Peking and Moscow*, pp. 100–104.

42. Wayne Kiyosaki, *North Korea's Foreign Relations: The Politics of Accommodation, 1945–1975* (New York: Praeger, 1976), p. 78.

43. Kiyosaki, *North Korea's Foreign Relations*, p. 71.

44. Chung, *P'yongyang Between Peking and Moscow*, p. 130.

45. Kiyosaki, *North Korea's Foreign Relations*, p. 83.

46. Kiyosaki, *North Korea's Foreign Relations*, p. 84.

47. Chong-Sik Lee, "Evolution of the Korean Worker's Party and the Rise of Kim Chong-il," in Scalapino and Kim, *North Korea Today*, p. 71.

48. Shim Jae Hoon, "Kith and Kim: President's Family to the Fore in Major Reshuffle," *Far Eastern Economic Review*, 23 December 1993, p. 25.

49. Morgan E. Clippinger, "Kim Chŏng-il in the North Korean Mass Media: A Study of Semi-esoteric Communication," *Asian Survey*, vol. 21, no. 3 (March 1981), pp. 289–309.

50. Byung Chul Koh, "The Cult of Personality and the Succession Issue," in C.I. Eugene Kim and B.C. Koh, eds., *Journey to North Korea: Personal Perceptions* (Berkeley: Institute of East Asian Studies, University of California, 1983), pp. 34–36.

51. Lee, "Evolution of the Korean Worker's Party," p. 75.

52. Mun Woong Lee, *Rural North Korea*, p. 73.

53. Suh, *Kim Il Sung*, p. 286.

54. Yi U-yong, "Kim Chong-il's Image as Reflected in North Korean Movies," *Sin Tong'a*, September 1994. Translated in Foreign Broadcast Information Service—East Asia, 19 October 1994, pp. 40–46.

55. Kim Jong Il, *The Art of the Cinema* (Pyongyang: Foreign Languages Publishing House, 1978).

56. Choe In Su, *Kim Jong Il, the People's Leader*, vol. 1 (Pyongyang: Foreign Languages Publishing House, 1983), pp. 2–6.

57. Charles K. Armstrong, "Centering the Periphery: Manchurian Exile(s) and the North Korean State," *Korean Studies*, no. 19 (1995), pp. 1–16.

58. *Hangyore Shinmun*, 12 July 1994. Translated in Foreign Broadcast Information Service-East Asia, 21 September 1994, pp. 60–61.

59. See Andrew Natsios, *The Great North Korean Famine: Famine, Politics, and Foreign Policy* (Washington, DC: United States Institute of Peace, 2001).

60. Charles K. Armstrong, "A Socialism of Our Style: North Korean Ideology in a Post-Communist Era," in Samuel S. Kim, ed., *North Korean Foreign Policy in the Post-Cold War Era* (Oxford, UK: Oxford University Press, 1998).

61. Paul Bracken, "The North Korean Nuclear Program as a Problem of State Survival," in Andrew Mack, ed., *Asian Flashpoint: Security and the Korean Peninsula* (New York: Allen & Unwin, 1993), p. 86.

62. Joseph S. Chung, "Economic Planning in North Korea," in Robert Scalapino and Jun-yop Kim, eds., *North Korea Today: Strategic and Domestic Issues* (Berkeley, CA: Institute of East Asian Studies, University of California, 1983), p. 176.

63. Samuel S. Kim, "North Korea and the Non-Communist World," in Chong-Sik Lee and Se-Hee Yoo, eds., *North Korea in Transition* (Berkeley, CA: Institute of East Asian Studies, University of California, 1991), p. 34.

64. Samuel S. Kim, "The Impact of the Division of Korea on South Korean Politics: The Challenge of Competitive Legitimation," paper presented at the Fifth International Conference on Korean Politics (Seoul, July 20, 1991), p. 30.

65. "Socialism Unites People with One Mind and One Will," *Korea Today*, January 1993, p. 5.

66. For the full text of the agreement, see *Korea Observer*, vol. 25, no. 4 (Winter 1994), pp. 597–600.

67. Selig S. Harrison, *Korean Endgame: A Strategy for Reunification and U.S. Disengagement* (Princeton, NJ: Princeton University Press, 2002), p. 25.

68. *Rodong Sinmun*, January 9, 2002, p. 1.

69. "Let us Examine and Solve all Problems from a New Perspective and Position," *Nodong Sinmun*, January 9, 2001.

70. Nam Kwang-sik, "One Year of a 'New Way of Thinking,'" *Vantage Point*, vol. 24, no. 2 (February 2002), p. 10.

71. *Rodong Sinmun*, January 1, 2002, p. 1; *People's Korea*, January 12, 2002, p. 2.

72. "SPA Approves New State Budget Featuring Technical Innovation and Modernization of Economy, *People's Korea*, March 30, 2002, p. 1.

73. "North Korea Undergoing Economic Reform," *Chosun Ilbo*, July 26, 2002; "Stitch by Stitch to a Different World," *The Economist*, July 27, 2002, pp. 24–26.

74. Howard W. French, "North Korea to Let Capitalism Loose in Investment Zone," *The New York Times*, September 25, 2002, p. A3.

75. "North Korea: Progress at a Snail's Pace," *The Economist*, October 11, 2003, p. 43.

76. Mark O'Neill, "Kim Jong Il Eyes New Chief Executive for Sinŭiju," *South China Morning Post*, September 10, 2004. CanKor No. 179. http://www.cankor.ligi.ubc.ca/ issues/179.htm.

77. "Let us Fully Demonstrate the Dignity and Power of the Republic under the Great Banner of Military-Based Policy," *Rodong Sinmun*, January 1, 2003, p. 1.

78. Ruediger Frank, "The End of Socialism and a Wedding Gift for the Groom? The True Meaning of Military First Policy," http://www.nautilus.org/DPRK BriefingBook/transition/Ruediger_Socialism.html.

CHAPTER FOUR

1. Bruce Cumings, *The Origins of the Korean War: Liberation and the Emergence of Separate Regimes, 1945–1947* (Princeton, NJ: Princeton University Press, 1981), p. 25.

2. Paul Gilroy, *The Black Atlantic: Modernity and Double Consciousness* (Cambridge, MA: Harvard University Press, 1993); Robin Cohen, *Global Diasporas: An Introduction* (Seattle, WA: University of Washington Press, 1997).

3. See Kwangkyu Lee, *Overseas Koreans* (Seoul: Jimoondang, 2001).

4. Khachang Toloyan, "The Nation-State and its Others: In Lieu of a Preface," *Diaspora: A Journal of Transnational Studies*, vol. 1, no. 1 (Spring 1991), p. 1; Chantal Bordes-Benayoun and Dominique Schnapper, *Diasporas et Nations* (Paris: Odile Jacob, 2006), p. 20.

5. Adam McKeown, "Global Migration, 1846–1940," *Journal of World History*, vol. 15, no. 2 (2004), pp. 2–3. http://www.historycooperative. org/journals/jwh/15.2/mckeown.html.

6. Sun Chunri, "The Formation of Korean Areas around Yanbian in Jilin Province," *Minzu Yanjiu* [Nationality Studies], January 1990, p. 87.

7. Han Sang-bok and Kwon T'ae-hwan, *Chungguk Yŏnbyŏnŭi Chosŏnjŏk* [The Korean Nationality of Yanbian, China] (Seoul: Seoul National University Press, 1993), p. 27; *Chosŏnjok ryaksa* [Brief History of the Korean Nationality] (Seoul: Paeksan sŏdang, 1989), p. 74.

8. Chae-Jin Lee, *China's Korean Minority: The Politics of Ethnic Education* (Boulder, CO: Westview Press, 1986), p. 17.

9. Louise Young, *Japan's Total Empire: Manchuria and the Culture of Wartime Imperialism* (Berkeley, CA: University of California Press, 1998), pp. 394–395.

10. See Byung-yool Ban, "Korean Emigration to the Russian Far East, 1860s–1910s." *Seoul Journal of Korean Studies*, vol. 9 (1996), pp. 115–143.

11. Haruki Wada, "Koreans in the Soviet Far East, 1917–1937," in Dae-Sook Suh, ed., *Koreans in the Soviet Union* (Honolulu: Center for Korean Studies, University of Hawaii, 1987).

12. Michael Gelb, "An Early Soviet Ethnic Deportation: The Far-Eastern Koreans," *The Russian Review*, vol. 54 (July 1995), pp. 389–412; Terry Martin, "The Origins of Soviet Ethnic Cleansing," *The Journal of Modern History*, vol. 70 (December 1998), pp. 833–836.

13. Gelb, "Ethnic Deportation," p. 390.

14. See Hahm Chae-bong, "Civilization, Race, or Nation? Korean Visions of Regional Order in the Late Nineteenth Century," in Charles K. Armstrong, Gilbert Rozman, Samuel Kim and Stephen Kotkin, eds., *Korea at the Center: Dynamics of Regionalism in Northeast Asia* (Armonk, NY: M.E. Sharpe, 2006), pp. 35–50.

15. Sonia Ryang, "The Great Kanto Earthquake and the Massacre of Koreans in 1923: Notes on Japan's Modern National Sovereignty," *Anthropological Quarterly*, vol. 76, no. 4 (Fall 2003), pp. 731–748.

16. Richard Hanks Mitchell, *The Korean Minority in Japan* (Berkeley, CA: University of California Press, 1967), p. 76.

17. Utsumi Aiko, "Korean 'Imperial Soldiers': Remembering Colonialism and Crimes against Allied POWS," in Tak Fujitani, Geoffrey M. White, Lisa Yoneyama, eds., *Perilous Memories: The Asia-Pacific War(s)* (Durham, NC: Duke University Press, 2001), pp. 199–217.

18. Yoshiaki Yoshimi, *Comfort Women: Sexual Slavery in the Japanese Military During World War II*, trans. Suzanne O'Brien (New York: Columbia University Press, 2000).

19. Some 10 percent of the atomic bomb victims in Hiroshima and Nagasaki—70,000 people—were Koreans. Most were laborers conscripted to work in the munitions plants, or landless farmers. Almost none received the compensation the Japanese government awarded Japanese atomic bomb victims. See Andreas Hippen, "The End of Silence: Korea's Hiroshima," *The Japan Times*, Aug. 2, 2005. http://search.japantimes.co.jp/print/features/life2005/fl20050802zg.htm, and Toyonaga Keisaburo, "Colonialism and Atom Bombs: About Survivors of Hiroshima Living in Korea," in Fujitani et al., eds., *Perilous Memories*, pp. 378–394.

20. See Wayne Patterson, *The Korean Frontier in America: Immigration to Hawaii, 1896–1910* (Honolulu: University of Hawaii Press, 1988), and Wayne Patterson, *The Ilse: First-Generation Korean Immigrants in Hawaii, 1903–1973* (Honolulu: University of Hawaii Press, 2000).

21. Nancy Abelmann and John Lie, *Blue Dreams: Korean Americans and the Los Angeles Riots* (Cambridge, MA: Harvard University Press, 1995), p. 99.

22. Yu Eui-Young estimates that approximately one-quarter of the 800,000 Koreans in the United States resided in Southern California in 1990. Cited in Abelmann and Lie, *Blue Dreams*, p. 81.

23. Cumings, *Origins of the Korean War*, Chapter 2.

24. John Lie, among others, had argued that Japan's myth of mono-ethnicity is largely a product of the postwar period. See Lie, *Multi-Ethnic Japan* (Cambridge, MA: Harvard University Press, 2001).

25. Mitchell, *Korean Minority in Japan*, pp. 102–104.

26. Sonia Ryang, *North Koreans in Japan: Language, Ideology, and Identity* (Boulder, CO: Westview Press, 1997).

27. Mitchell, *Korean Minority in Japan*, p. 136.

28. See *Korean Returnees from Japan* (Pyongyang: Foreign Languages Publishing House, 1960).

29. This is the experience of Kang Ch'ŏl-hwan, who migrated to North Korea from Japan with his family and ended up in a labor camp (the entire family included) for ten years, beginning at the age of nine. Kang Chol-hwan [Kang Ch'ŏl-hwan] and Pierre Rigoulot, *The Aquariums of Pyong-yang: Ten Years in the North Korean Gulag* (New York: Basic Books, 2001).

30. See *If I Had Wings Like a Bird I Would Fly Across the Sea: Letters from the Japanese Wives of North Korea Repatriates* (New York: The American Committee for Human Rights of Japanese Wives of North Korean Repatriates, 1974).

31. I happened to be on the same flight from Pyongyang to Beijing as the Japanese spouses; the women were almost entirely silent for the duration of the flight.

32. *Time Magazine*, June 13, 1994. Cited in Bruce Cumings, *Korea's Place in the Sun: A Modern History* (New York: W. W. Norton, 2005), p. 341. Cumings believes the actual total to be much higher.

33. Chikako Kashiwazaki, "To Be Korean Without Korean Nationality: Claim to Korean Identity by Japanese Nationality Holders," *Korean and Korean American Studies Bulletin*, vol. 11, no. 1 (2000), pp. 48–70.

34. Charles K. Armstrong, *The North Korean Revolution, 1945–1950* (Ithaca, NY: Cornell University Press, 2003), Chapter 1.

35. Bernard Vincent Olivier, "Korean Contributions to the Development of Heilongjiang/ Hongnyonggang," *Korea Journal*, vol. 35, no. 4 (Winter 1995), pp. 54–71.

36. Michael J. Seth, *Education Fever: Society, Politics, and the Pursuit of Schooling in South Korea* (Honolulu: University of Hawaii Press, 2002).

37. Andrei Lankov, *Crisis in North Korea: The Failure of De-Stalinization, 1956* (Honolulu: University of Hawaii Press, 2005).

38. German Kim, "The History, Culture and Language of the Koryŏ Saram," *Korea Journal*, vol. 33, no. 1 (Spring 1993), p. 47.

39. Jun Kwan-woo, "Sticky Issue of Resettlement," *Newsreview* [Seoul], October 17, 1998, p. 7. The plight of the Koreans of Sakhalin is powerfully described in DaiSil Kim-Gibson's documentary "A Forgotten People: The Sakhalin Koreans" (1995).

40. Abelmann and Lie, *Blue Dreams*, p. 67.

41. Elaine H. Kim, "Home is Where the Han Is: A Korean-American Perspective on the Los Angeles Upheavals," in Robert Gooding-Williams, ed., *Reading Rodney King/Reading Urban Uprising* (New York: Routledge, 1993), p. 219.

42. Edward Taehan Chang, "The Post-Los Angeles Riot Korean American Community: Challenges and Prospects," *Korean and Korean American Studies Bulletin* vol. 10, no. 1 (1999), p. 11.

43. Chang, "Post-Los Angeles Riots," p. 13.

44. "Adopter of 8 Koreans Off to Get 200 More," *The New York Times*, March 26, 1956, p. 6.

45. For documents on the Korean "Operation Baby-Lift"—precursor of the more famous Operation Baby Lift of the Vietnam War—see United States National Archives and Records Administration, Record Group 319. Records of the Army Staff, Box 29. Records of the Office of the Chief of Civilian Affairs, Correspondence of the Public Affairs Division, 1950–1964.

46. Key P. Yang and Chang Bo Chee, "North Korean Education System, 1945 to Present," *China Quarterly*, no. 14 (1963), p. 128.

47. Koreans use both the term *moguk* ("mother country") and *choguk* ("fatherland," literally "ancestral country") to refer to Korea. First-generation immigrants often use the term *uri nara* ("our country"), but this tends to change as later generations feel less attachment to Korea as "their" country.

48. Suji Kwock Kim, "Translations from my Mother Tongue," *Notes from the Divided Country* (Baton Rouge, LA: Louisiana State University Press, 2003), p. 16.

CHAPTER FIVE

1. The South Korean literary critic Paik Nak-chung has dubbed this Korea's "division system"—the two Koreas existing in a strange hostile dependency that has been used to justify repression in both regimes, at least until recently. Paik Nak-chung, "South Korea: Unification and the Democratic Challenge," *New Left Review*, no. 197 (January–February 1993), pp. 67–84.

2. For an elaboration of this four-stage view of inter-Korean relations, see Charles K. Armstrong, "Inter-Korean Relations in Historical Perspective," *International Journal of Korean Unification Studies*, vol. 14, no. 2 (December 2005), pp. 1–20.

3. Syngman Rhee was quite explicit about his desire to invade and conquer the North, both before and after the Korean War. At least until the late 1950s, the United States took these threats seriously and had detailed contingency plans (code-named Operation USAKOM) in case of a South Korean invasion.

4. Annette Baker Fox, *The Power of Small States: Diplomacy in World War II* (Chicago, IL: University of Chicago Press, 1959).

5. Constantine Pleshakov, "Nikita Khrushchev and Sino-Soviet Relations," in Odd Arne Westad, ed., *Brothers in Arms: The Rise and Fall of the Sino-Soviet Alliance, 1945–1963* (Stanford, CA: Stanford University Press, 1998), p. 234.

6. Chen and Yang, "Chinese Politics and the Collapse of the Sino Soviet Alliance," in Westad, ed., *Brothers in Arms*, p. 268.

7. Vladislav M. Zubok, "The Khrushchev-Mao Conversations, 31 July–3 August 1958 and 2 October 1958," *Cold War International History Project Bulletin*, nos. 12 and 13 (Fall/Winter 2001), p. 245.

8. David Wolff, "'One Finger's Worth of Historical Events': New Russian and Chinese Evidence on the Sino-Soviet Alliance and Split, 1948–1959," *Cold War International History Project Working Paper No. 30*, August 2000, p. 14.

9. Soviet Embassy in DPRK, Report, 28 November 1960. Foreign Policy Archive of the Russian Federation (AVPRF), Fond 0102, Opis 16, Papka 85, Delo 7.

10. Cited in Chin O. Chung, *P'yongyang Between Peking and Moscow: North Korea's Involvement in the Sino-Soviet Dispute, 1958–1975* (Tuscaloosa, AL: University of Alabama Press, 1978), p. 65.

11. According to the recollection of one of the Soviet delegates, cited in Zubok, "The Mao-Khrushchev Conversations," p. 247.

12. Soviet Embassy in DPRK, Report, December 16, 1959. AVPRF, Fond 0102, Opis 15, Papka 81, Delo 7.

13. Soviet Embassy in DPRK, Report, October 7, 1959. AVPRF, Fond 0102, Opis 15, Papka 81, Delo 7.

14. Chung, *P'yongyang Between Peking and Moscow*, pp. 68–80.

15. Chae-Jin Lee, *China's Korean Minority: The Politics of Ethnic Education* (Boulder, CO: Westview, 1986), p. 87.

16. Soviet Embassy in DPRK, Report, August 1962. AVPRF, Fond 0102, Opis 16, Papka 87, Delo 29.

17. Chung, *P'yongyang Between Peking and Moscow*, p. 56.

18. Chung, *P'yongyang Between Peking and Moscow*, pp. 56–57.

19. Soviet Embassy in DPRK, Report, April 5, 1962. AVPRF, Fond 0102, Opis 16, Papka 87, Delo 29.

20. Michael Schaller, *The American Occupation of Japan: The Origins of the Cold War in Asia* (New York: Oxford University Press, 1985); Bruce Cumings, "The Origins and Development of the Northeast Asian Political Economy," *International Organization*, vol. 38, no. 1 (Winter 1984), pp. 1–40.

21. Barry K. Gills, *Korea versus Korea: A Case of Contested Legitimacy* (London: Routledge, 1996), pp. 109–110.

22. Chuck Downs, "Discerning North Korea's Intentions," in Nicholas Eberstadt and Richard J. Ellings, ed., *Korea's Future and the Great Powers* (Seattle, WA: The National Bureau of Asian Research, 2001), p. 96.

23. B.C. Koh, "A Comparison of Unification Policies," in Young Whan Kihl, ed., *Korea and the World: Beyond the Cold War* (Boulder, CO: Westview Press, 1994), p. 156.

24. Selig Harrison, *Korean Endgame: A Strategy for Reunification and US Disengagement* (Princeton, NJ: Princeton University Press, 2002), p. 76.

25. "The Politics of Inter-Korean Relations: Coexistence or Reunification," in Kihl, ed., *Korea and the World*, p. 135.

26. See for example Nick Eberstadt, *The End of North Korea* (Washington, DC: AEI Press, 1999).

27. Fifteen years after the disintegration of the USSR, it may seem that the "collapse of communism" was overrated. Arguably this was a regional (European) rather than global event: of the fifteen Marxist-Leninist regimes that existed in 1989, ten had disappeared within two years, while five (China, North Korea, Vietnam, Laos, and Cuba) remain with us today. It is worth noting that four of the five are in eastern Asia.

28. North Korea and Saddam Hussein's Iraq were the only "evil regimes" singled out by name in the Bush Administration's major policy statement of September 2002, *The National Security Strategy of the United States of America* (Falls Village, CT: Winterhouse Editions, 2002), Section Five.

29. "A Socialism of Our Style: North Korean Ideology in a Post-Communist Era," in Samuel S. Kim, ed., *North Korean Foreign Policy in the Post-Cold War Era* (Oxford, UK: Oxford University Press, 1998).

30. Paul Bracken, "The North Korean Nuclear Program as a Problem of State Survival," in Andrew Mack, ed., *Asian Flashpoint: Security and the Korean Peninsula* (New York: Allen & Unwin, 1993), p. 86.

31. See Leon V. Sigal, *Disarming Strangers: Nuclear Diplomacy with North Korea* (Princeton, NJ: Princeton University Press, 1998).

32. Valery I. Denisov, "Nuclear Institutions and Organizations in North Korea," in James Clay Moltz and Alexandre Y. Mansourov, eds., *The North Korean Nuclear Program: Security Strategy and New Perspectives from Russia,* (London: Routledge, 2000), p. 21.

33. While the oft-repeated CIA estimate was that North Korea had the material for "one or two" nuclear weapons, Russian experts at the time believed that North Korea did not have the technology to build nuclear weapons, even if they possessed sufficient weapons-grade plutonium. Ibid., p. 25.

34. Samuel S. Kim, "North Korea in 2000," *Asian Survey,* vol. 41, no. 1 (January/ February 2001), p. 20.

35. "North Korea Undergoing Economic Reform," *The Chosun Ilbo,* July 26, 2002; "Stitch by Stitch to a Different World," *The Economist,* July 27, 2002, pp. 24–26.

36. "DPRK Denounces Bush's Charges: Statement of FM Spokesman on Bush's State of the Union Address," *People's Korea,* February 9, 2002, p. 1.

37. "Inter-Korean Festival Kicks Off in Seoul," *Korea Times,* August 14, 2002, p. 1.

38. "Work Starts on North Korea's U.S.-Backed Nuclear Plant," *New York Times,* August 8, 2002, p. A14.

39. Howard W. French, "North Koreans Sign Agreement with Japanese," *New York Times,* September 18, 2002, p. A1.

40. U.S. State Department Press Statement, "North Korean Nuclear Program," October 16, 2002. http://www.state.gov/r/pa/prs/ps/2002/14423pf/htm.

41. "Pyongyang Hits Seoul's Decision to Dispatch Troops to Iraq," *People's Korea,* April 22, 2003, p. 1.

42. "North, South Conclude 7-Point Agreement in Inter-Korean Economic Talks," *People's Korea*, May 31, 2003, p. 1.

43. "Fifth Meeting of North-South Committee for Promotion of Economic Cooperation Concludes," *Chosŏn t'ongsin (Korea Central News Agency)*, May 24, 2003. http://www.kcna.co.jp/index-k.htm.

44. http://www.kcna.co.jp/index-e.htm, 11 February 2005.

45. An Sang Nam, "Why North Korea Isn't Talking," *Asian Times*, June 11, 2005. http://atimesol.atimes.com/atimes/archives/6_11.2005.html.

46. Joel Brinkley, "South Korea Offers Power if North Quits Arms Program," *The New York Times*, July 13, 2005, p. A6.

47. Joel Brinkley, "Setting the Table for North Korea's Return," *The New York Times*, July 11, 2005; http://www.nytimes.com/2005/07/11/international/asia/11assess.htm.

48. Jim Yardley and David E. Sanger, "U.S. Tries a New Approach in Talks with North Korea," *New York Times*, July 27, 2005, p. A10.

49. "Full Text of Joint Statement from Six-Way Nuclear Talks," *Vantage Point*, October 2005, p. 11.

50. Joseph Kahn, "North Korea and U.S. Spar, Causing Talks to Stall," *New York Times*, November 12, 2005, p. A6.

51. See Roland Bleiker, *Divided Korea: Toward a Culture of Reconciliation* (Minneapolis, MN: University of Minnesota Press, 2005) and Roy Richard Grinker, *Korea and its Futures: Unification and the Unfinished War* (New York: St. Martin's Press, 1998).

52. Gregory Henderson, Richard Ned Lebow, and John G. Stoessinger, eds., *Divided Nations in a Divided World* (New York, D. McKay Co., 1974).

CHAPTER SIX

1. The Korean-Chinese (*Huaqiao*, or Hwagyo in Korean pronunciation), mostly descendents of immigrants from Shandong Province across the Yellow Sea who arrived in the late nineteenth century, were until recently the largest nonethnic Korean community in both North and South Korea. After liberation, many left Korea for mainland China or Taiwan. Ironically, Korean-Chinese have long faced economic discrimination and prejudice in South Korea not unlike that of the Koreans in Japan, although the two histories are very different.

2. E.J. Hobsbawm, *Nations and Nationalism Since 1780: Programme, Myth, Reality* (Cambridge, UK: Cambridge University Press, 1990); Benedict Anderson, *Imagined Communities: Reflections on the Origin and Spread of Nations* (New York: Verso, 1983).

3. Henry Em, "Minjok as a Modern and Democratic Concept," in Gi-wook Shin and Michael Robinson, eds., *Colonial Modernity in Korea* (Cambridge, MA: Harvard University Asia Center, Distributed by Harvard University Press, 1999), pp. 336–361.

4. Perhaps all nations are fragmentary; this is certainly the case for India, admittedly a very different nation-state from Korea, as Partha Chatterjee has argued in *The Nation and Its Fragments* (Princeton, NJ: Princeton University Press, 1993).

5. Ian Clark, *Globalization and Fragmentation: International Relations in the Twentieth Century* (Oxford, UK: Oxford University Press, 1997).

6. On historical and contemporary regionalism, see *La Corée en Miettes* [Korea in Pieces], special issue of *Revue Géographie et Cultures*, no. 51 (Autumn 2004), ed. Valérie Gelézeau.

7. Katherine H.S. Moon, "Strangers in the Midst of Globalization: Migrant Workers and Korean Nationalism," in Samuel S. Kim, ed., *Korea's Globalization* (New York: Cambridge University Press, 2000).

8. Many interview studies of defectors have reported this. I participated in one such study in 2000, an extensive interview with five male North Korean refugees sponsored by Yonsei University in Seoul. All five had done reasonably well in South Korea but were still irked by South Korean prejudices and felt treated as "other."

9. Roy Richard Grinker, *Korea and its Futures: Unification and the Unfinished War* (New York: St. Martin's Press, 1998).

10. Choi Jang-jip, *Democracy after Democratization: The Korean Experience*, trans. Lee Kyung-hee (Seoul: Humanitas, 2005).

Bibliography

Abelmann, Nancy and John Lie. *Blue Dreams: Korean Americans and the Los Angeles Riots* (Cambridge: Harvard University Press, 1995).

Amsden, Alice. *Asia's Next Giant: South Korea and Late Industrialization* (Oxford, UK: Oxford University Press, 1989).

Anderson, Benedict. *Imagined Communities: Reflections on the Origin and Spread of Nations* (New York: Verso, 1983).

Armstrong, Charles K. *The North Korean Revolution, 1945–1950* (Ithaca, NY: Cornell University Press, 2003).

Armstrong, Charles K., Gilbert Rozman, Samuel S. Kim, and Stephen Kotkin, eds. *Korea at the Center: Dynamics of Regionalism in Northeast Asia* (Armonk, NY: M.E. Sharpe, 2006).

Bleiker, Roland. *Divided Korea: Toward a Culture of Reconciliation* (Minneapolis, MN: University of Minnesota Press, 2005).

Bordes-Benayoun, Chantal and Dominique Schnapper. *Diasporas et Nations* (Paris: Odile Jacob, 2006).

Brun, Ellen and Jacques Hersh. *Socialist Korea: A Case Study of the Strategy of Economic Development* (New York: Monthly Review Press, 1976).

Ch'oe, Yongho, Peter H. Lee and Wm. Theodore de Bary, eds. *Source of Korean Tradition, Vol. 2: From the Sixteenth to the Twentieth Centuries* (New York: Columbia University Press, 2000).

Chandra, Vipan. *Imperialism, Resistance, and Reform in Late Nineteenth-Century Korea: Enlightenment and the Independence Club* (Berkeley: Institute of East Asian Studies, University of California, Berkeley, Center for Korean Studies, 1988).

Chatterjee, Partha. *Nationalist Thought and the Colonial World: A Derivative Discourse?* (London: Zed Books, 1986).

Chatterjee, Partha. *The Nation and Its Fragments* (Princeton, NJ: Princeton University Press, 1993).

Choi, Jang-jip. *Democracy After Democratization: The Korean Experience* trans. Lee Kyung-hee (Seoul: Humanitas, 2005).

Chung, Chin O. *P'yongyang between Peking and Moscow: North Korea's Involvement in the Sino-Soviet Dispute, 1958–1975* (Tuscaloosa, AL: University of Alabama Press, 1978).

Clark, Ian. *Globalization and Fragmentation: International Relations in the Twentieth Century* (Oxford, UK: Oxford University Press, 1997).

Clough, Ralph N. *Embattled Korea: The Rivalry for International Support* (Boulder, CO: Westview Press, 1987).

Cohen, Robin. *Global Diasporas: An Introduction* (Seattle, WA: University of Washington Press, 1997).

Cumings, Bruce. "The Origins and Development of the Northeast Asian Political Economy," *International Organization*, vol. 38, no. 1 (Winter 1984), pp. 1–40.

Cumings, Bruce. *Korea's Place in the Sun: A Modern History* (New York: W. W. Norton, 2005).

Cumings, Bruce. *The Origins of the Korean War: Liberation and the Emergence of Separate Regimes, 1945–1947* (Princeton, NJ: Princeton University Press, 1981).

Duncan, John B. *Origins of the Chosŏn Dynasty* (Seattle, WA: University of Washington Press, 2000).

Duus, Peter. *The Abacus and the Sword: The Japanese Penetration of Korea, 1895–1910* (Berkeley, CA: University of California Press, 1995).

Eberstadt, Nicholas and Richard J. Ellings, eds. *Korea's Future and the Great Powers* (Seattle, WA: The National Bureau of Asian Research, 2001).

Eberstadt, Nick. *The End of North Korea* (Washington, DC: AEI Press, 1999).

Eckert, Carter J. *Offspring of Empire: The Koch'ang Kims and the Colonial Origins of Korean Capitalism, 1876–1945* (Seattle, WA: University of Washington Press, 1991).

Fox, Annette Baker. *The Power of Small States: Diplomacy in World War II* (Chicago, IL: University of Chicago Press, 1959).

Fujitani, Tak, Geoffrey M. White and Lisa Yoneyama, eds. *Perilous Memories: The Asia-Pacific War(s)* (Durham, NC: Duke University Press, 2001).

Gelb, Michael. "An Early Soviet Ethnic Deportation: The Far-Eastern Kore-
    ans," *The Russian Review,* vol. 54 (July 1995), pp. 389–412.

Gills, Barry K. *Korea versus Korea: A Case of Contested Legitimacy* (London: Rout-
    ledge, 1996).

Gilroy, Paul. *The Black Atlantic: Modernity and Double Consciousness* (Cambridge,
    MA: Harvard University Press, 1993).

Grinker, Roy Richard. *Korea and its Futures: Unification and the Unfinished War* (New
    York: St. Martin's Press, 1998).

Held, David, Anthony G. McGrew, David Goldblatt, and Jonathan Perraton.
    Global Transformations: Politics, Economics and Culture (Stanford, CA: Stanford
    University Press, 1995).

Henderson, Gregory, Richard Ned Lebow and John G. Stoessinger, eds.
    Divided Nations in a Divided World (New York: D. McKay Co., 1974).

Hobsbawm, E.J. *Nations and Nationalism Since 1780: Programme, Myth, Reality* (Cam-
    bridge, UK: Cambridge University Press, 1990).

Johnson, Chalmers. *Blowback: The Costs and Consequences of American Empire* (New
    York: Henry Holt & Co., 2000).

Kang Chol-hwan and Pierre Rigoulot. *The Aquariums of Pyongyang: Ten Years in the
    North Korean Gulag,* trans. Yair Reiner (New York: Basic Books, 2001).

Kihl, Young Whan, ed. *Korea and the World: Beyond the Cold War* (Boulder, CO:
    Westview Press, 1994).

Kim, Eun Mee. *Big Business, Strong State: Collusion and Conflict in South Korean Development,
    1960–1990* (Albany, NY: State University of New York Press, 1997).

Kim, Linsu. *Imitation to Innovation: The Dynamics of Korea's Technological Learning*
    (Boston, MA: Harvard Business School Press, 1997).

Kim, Samuel S., ed. *Korea's Democratization* (Cambridge, UK: Cambridge Uni-
    versity Press, 2003).

Kim, Samuel S., ed. *Korea's Globalization* (New York: Cambridge University
    Press, 2000).

Kim, Samuel S., ed. *North Korean Foreign Policy in the Post-Cold War Era* (Oxford,
    UK: Oxford University Press, 1998).

Kim, Sunhyuk. *The Politics of Democratization in Korea: The Role of Civil Society* (Pitts-
    burgh, PA: University of Pittsburgh Press, 2000).

Kiyosaki, Wayne. *North Korea's Foreign Relations: The Politics of Accommodation, 1945–
    1975* (New York: Praeger, 1976).

Koo, Hagen. *Korean Workers: The Culture and Politics of Class Formation* (Ithaca, NY: Cornell University Press, 2001).

Lankov, Andrei. *Crisis in North Korea: The Failure of De-Stalinization, 1956* (Honolulu: University of Hawaii Press, 2005).

Ledyard, Gari. *The Dutch Come to Korea*. (Seoul: Royal Asiatic Society, Korea Branch, 1971).

Lee, Jai-eui. *Kwangju Diary: Beyond Death, Beyond the Darkness of the Age*, trans. Kap Su Seol and Nick Mamatas (Los Angeles, CA: UCLA Asia Pacific Monograph Series, 1999).

Lee, Chae-Jin. *China's Korean Minority: The Politics of Ethnic Education* (Boulder, CO: Westview Press, 1986).

Lensen, George Alexander. *Balance of Intrigue: International Rivalry in Korea and Manchuria, 1884–1899* (Tallahassee, FL: University Press of Florida, 1982).

Leung, Anthony. *Korean Cinema: The New Hong Kong* (London: Trafford, 2003).

Lewis, Martin W. and Karin Wigen. *The Myth of Continents: A Critique of Metageography* (Berkeley, CA: University of California Press, 1997).

Lie, John. *Multi-Ethnic Japan* (Cambridge, MA: Harvard University Press, 2001).

Mansourov, Alexandre Y. "Communist War Coalition Formation and the Origins of the Korean War." Ph.D. dissertation, Columbia University, NY, 1997.

McKeown, Adam. "Global Migration, 1846–1940," *Journal of World History*, vol. 15, no. 2 (2004).

Merrill, John. *Korea: The Peninsular Origins of the War* (Newark, NJ: University of Delaware Press, 1989).

Mitchell, Richard Hanks. *The Korean Minority in Japan* (Berkeley, CA: University of California Press, 1967).

Moltz, James Clay and Alexandre Y. Mansourov, eds. *The North Korean Nuclear Program: Security Strategy and New Perspectives from Russia* (London: Routledge, 2000).

Nam, Koon Woo. *The North Korean Communist Leadership, 1945–1965: A Study of Factionalism and Political Consolidation* (Tuscaloosa, AL: University of Alabama Press, 1974).

Natsios, Andrew. *The Great North Korean Famine: Famine, Politics, and Foreign Policy* (Washington, DC: United States Institute of Peace, 2001).

Nelson, Laura. *Measured Excess: Status, Gender and Consumer Nationalism in South Korea* (New York: Columbia University Press, 2000).

Noland, Marcus. *Avoiding the Apocalypse: The Future of the Two Koreas* (Washington, DC: Institute for International Economics, 2000).

O Tuathail, Gearoid. *Critical Geopolitics: The Politics of Writing Global Space* (Minneapolis, MN: University of Minnesota Press, 1996).

Oberdorfer, Don. *The Two Koreas: A Contemporary History* (Reading, MA: Addison-Wesley, 1997).

Ogle, George E. *South Korea: Dissent Within the Economic Miracle* (London: Zed Books, 1990).

Pai, Hyung Il. *Constructing "Korean" Origins: A Critical Review of Archaeology, Historiography, and Racial Myth in Korean State-Formation Theories* (Cambridge, MA: Harvard University East Asia Series, 2000).

Palais, James. *Confucian Statecraft and Korean Institutions: Yu Hyŏngwŏn and the Late Chosŏn Dynasty* (Seattle, WA: University of Washington Press, 1996).

Palais, James. *Politics and Policy in Traditional Korea* (Cambridge, MA: Harvard University Press, 1975).

Patterson, Wayne. *The Ilse: First-Generation Korean Immigrants in Hawaii, 1903–1973* (Honolulu: University of Hawaii Press, 2000).

Patterson, Wayne. *The Korean Frontier in America: Immigration to Hawaii, 1896–1910* (Honolulu: University of Hawaii Press, 1988).

Ryang, Sonia. *North Koreans in Japan: Language, Ideology, and Identity* (Boulder, CO: Westview Press, 1997).

Scalapino, Robert and Chong S. Lee. *Communism in Korea*, 2 vols. (Berkeley, CA: University of California Press, 1972).

Schaller, Michael. *The American Occupation of Japan: The Origins of the Cold War in Asia* (New York: Oxford University Press, 1985).

Schmid, Andre. *Korea Between Empires, 1895–1919* (New York: Columbia University Press, 2002).

Scott-Stokes, Henry and Jai-eui Lee, eds. *The Kwangju Uprising: Eyewitness Press Accounts of Korea's Tiananmen* (Armonk, NY: M.E. Sharpe, 2000).

Seth, Michael J. *Education Fever: Society, Politics, and the Pursuit of Schooling in South Korea* (Honolulu: University of Hawaii Press, 2002).

Shin, Gi-wook and Kyung Moon Hwang, eds. *Contentious Kwangju: The May 18th Uprising in Korea's Past and Present* (Lanham, MD: Rowman & Littlefield, 2003).

Shin, Gi-wook and Michael Robinson, eds. *Colonial Modernity in Korea* (Cambridge, MA: Harvard University Asia Center, 1999).

Steinberg, David I., ed. *Korean Attitudes Toward the United States: Changing Dynamics* (Armonk, NY: M.E. Sharpe, 2004).

Stiglitz, Joseph. *Globalization and its Discontents* (New York: Norton, 2002).

Suh, Dae-Sook, ed. *Koreans in the Soviet Union* (Honolulu: Center for Korean Studies, University of Hawaii, 1987).

Suh, Dae-Sook. *Kim Il Sung, the North Korean Leader* (New York: Columbia University Press, 1988).

Un, Lim. *The Founding of a Dynasty in North Korea: An Authentic Biography of Kim Il Sung* (Tokyo: Jiyu-sha, 1982).

Weems, Benjamin. *Reform, Rebellion, and the Heavenly Way* (Tucson, AZ: University of Arizona Press, 1964).

Wells, Kenneth, ed. *South Korea's Minjung Movement: The Culture and Politics of Dissidence* (Honolulu: University of Hawaii Press, 1995).

Westad, Odd Arne, ed. *Brothers in Arms: The Rise and Fall of the Sino-Soviet Alliance, 1945–1963* (Stanford, CA: Stanford University Press, 1998).

Wolff, David. "'One Finger's Worth of Historical Events:' New Russian and Chinese Evidence on the Sino-Soviet Alliance and Split, 1948–1959," *Cold War International History Project Working Paper No. 30* (August 2000).

Woo, Jung-en. *Race to the Swift: State and Finance in Korean Industrialization* (New York: Columbia University Press, 1991).

Yoshimi, Yoshiaki. *Comfort Women: Sexual Slavery in the Japanese Military During World War II*, trans. Suzanne O'Brien (New York: Columbia University Press, 2000).

Young, Louise. *Japan's Total Empire: Manchuria and the Culture of Wartime Imperialism* (Berkeley, CA: University of California Press, 1998).

Zubok, Vladislav M. "The Khrushchev-Mao Conversations, 31 July–3 August 1958 and 2 October 1958," *Cold War International History Project Bulletin*, nos. 12 and 13 (Fall/Winter 2001).

Index

economy
North Korean, 5
disaster of, 79–84
restructuring of, 84–88
slowdown of, 70–71
South Korean, 2
dependence of, on U.S., 24
as hub, 52
rise, fall, and recovery of, 31–33
education system, South Korean, 24
emigration. *See* Korean diaspora
ethnic diversity, 48–49
exports, 29–30

F

famine, 80
farming collectives, 65
Federation of Korean Trade Unions, 39
film industry, 26, 49–50
financial crisis, of 1997, 28, 32–33
foreign adoptions, 123–27
foreign aid
to North Korea, 63–64
to South Korea, 24
foreign interactions, 11–12
foreign invasions, 6–8
Framework Agreement, 80, 83, 150–55, 156
France, imperialism of, 12

G

gender relationships, in South Korea, 48
generational differences, in South Korea, 45–46

geographic significance, 8–10, 52–53
geopolitical rivalry, 9–10, 14–17
German unification, 2, 16–17, 81–82, 161, 163
G.I. brides, 119
globalization, 1–2, 132
defined, 4
history of, 4–5
Korea and, 3–6
North Korea and, 163–64
South Korea and, 3–4
Grand National Party, 43, 45
grass-roots politics, in South Korea, 41–42
gross domestic product (GDP), 33, 50
gross national product (GNP), 31

H

Hallyu, 49–50
Hawaii, Korean emigration to, 102
Held, David, 4
Hermit Kingdom, 12–13, 89
Hill, Christopher, 158, 159–60
Holt, Henry, 124

I

Immigration Act (1924), 102–3, 119
imperialism, 12–13
See also Japanese colonization
Independence Club, 34
industrialization, in South Korea, 28–31, 47–48
industry, nationalization of, in North Korea, 65–66